CRITIQUE OF THE FOUNDATIONS OF PSYCHOLOGY

CRITIQUE
OF THE
FOUNDATIONS
OF
PSYCHOLOGY

THE PSYCHOLOGY OF PSYCHOANALYSIS

by Georges Politzer

translated by Maurice Apprey

Foreword by Amedeo Giorgi

DUQUESNE UNIVERSITY PRESS
Pittsburgh, Pennsylvania

Published by

DUQUESNE UNIVERSITY PRESS
600 Forbes Avenue
Pittsburgh, Pennsylvania 15282-0101

Library of Congress Cataloging-in-Publication Data

Politzer, Georges, 1903–1942.
   [Critique des fondements de la psychologie. English]
   Critique of the foundations of psychology : the psychology of
psychoanalysis / by Georges Politzer : translated by Maurice Apprey :
foreword by Amedeo Giorgi.
       p.   cm.
   Includes bibliographical references and index.
   ISBN 0-8207-0256-0 (cloth)   —   ISBN 0-8207-0257-9 (paper)

   1. Psychoanalysis—Philosophy. 2. Psychology—Philosophy.
3. Concrete (Philosophy)   I. Title
   [DNLM: 1. Psychoanalytic Theory. 2. Psychology. 3. Unconscious
(Psychology)   WM 460 P769c 1994a]
BF175.P   1994
150.19'5—dc20
DNLM/DLC
for Library of Congress   94-4139
                                          CIP

This translation is dedicated to the memory of

Mrs. Charlotte Balkanyi,
a psychoanalyst who intuitively understood
the work of Georges Politzer

and to

Effie Thelma Quagrainie

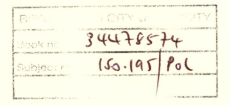

Contents

Acknowledgments

I am grateful to Françoise Laye of Presses Universitaires de France for permission to publish the English translation and for her continued enthusiasm for this project.

Gratitude is also due to John Dowds, director, and Susan Wadsworth-Booth, senior editor, of Duquesne University Press; and to Cornelia Robart, the bilingual copyeditor for the project, all of whom fostered a successful collaboration. Lina DiBlaso, a psychology graduate assistant of Professor Amedeo Giorgi and Elisabeth Harvey made significant editorial contributions to early drafts of the translation.

TRANSLATOR'S NOTE

Quite simply, why have I bothered to go through the agony of translating Georges Politer's Critique? Politzer's *Critique* has been translated into all major Western languages except English, but more importantly, French psychoanalysis and modern Continental philosophy cannot be easily understood without grasping Politzer's *concrete psychology* that, inter alia, eliminates the distinction between manifest contents and latent contents of mental life. There is thus one field of consciousness in Politzer's psychology. His influence is almost everywhere in modern French thought. It is an implicit or explicit foundation. His concrete psychology is thus a pre-text that informs elements of the work of the French philosopher, Maurice Merleau-Ponty, the work of psychoanalysts, Jacques Lacan, Jean Laplanche, Serge Leclaire, and many other French scholars.

It is probably quite safe to say that Politzer's concrete psychology is a common ground that the French have taken for granted. For that reason, French psychoanalytic thinkers have until now, at least implicitly, spoken to Politzer's phenomenology, whereas the rest of us have, more or less, remained faithful to versions of Freud that are relatively drained of the first-person drama. The English translation of Politzer's *Critique* will break down barriers that have hitherto constituted one obstacle to progress in psychoanalytic thought. Those barriers to progress, however, will not be removed without controversy, especially between those with a primarily intersubjectivist view and those who are committed structuralists.

In this translation, I have tried to be faithful to the language of the original text, while still making a readable contemporary version available in English. Certain conventions present in the original, such as Politzer's use of masculine pronouns in speaking of case studies and persons in general, have been retained.

Maurice Apprey

The Determinate Meaning of Dream Acts: A Reinterpretation of Freud's Metapsychology in Politzer's *Critique des Fondements de la Psychologie*

Maurice Apprey

Georges Politzer (1903–1942) was born in northeastern Hungary. At the age of 17, he settled in France to avoid persecution against his family. Politzer was a Marxist-philosopher whose dissertation on Bergson critiqued idealist philosophy.

Following the Nazi invasion of France, Politzer became a resistor to the occupation, emerging as a leading French spokesman for communism. Today, and mostly in France, he is known for his books *Critiques des Fondements de la Psychologie* and *La Crise de la Psychologie Contemporaine*, both of which critique Freud and Wundt. The second book has now been reissued as *Ecrits 2*.

Politzer was a man of conviction. In this respect he was consistent until the moment of his death at the hands of Gestapo in 1942 when he was in the forefront of the resistance. He held humanity responsible for its history, for its ideas, and for its dreams. For Politzer, human beings make their own history regardless of the consequences. Individual persons follow their own consciously desired ends. Like Engels, Politzer took the position that it was precisely the result of these many wills operating in different directions and of their manifold effects upon the external world that history is made.

Humankind is thus the motor of history; people act according to their ideas. Action creates history because history is determined by the will of human beings.

Just as Politzer saw history as the work of people whose actions came about because they had ideas, dreams possessed a first-person drama, too. Politzer was averse to any semblance of abstraction that concealed the meaning of the subject's creation of the dream. For Politzer, the meaning of the dream was synonymous with the latent content. The meaning of the dream is the author's intention, and the dream must not be subjected to abstraction. The dreams are actions that reveal the motivation of their maker. They are a first-person drama; they are *dream acts*, as it were.

Politzer's Criticism of Freud's "Realism"

Politzer's views are clear on this subject. For him, dream analysis does not move from manifest to latent content. Rather, a dream has only one content — the latent content, just as we can say that there is only one narrative. In addition, the dream expresses those meanings that have not found an adequate sign. For Politzer, dream interpretation is a simultaneous translation and the dream's meaning may not be expressed in the language of waking life. Instead, explanation must be symmetrical with the level of meaning.

Politzer's Criticism of Freud's "Abstraction"

The promise of Freud's early psychology (before he fell back into abstraction) was that it would replace impersonal mechanisms with a method for explaining dreams as acts of a particular subject with a particular desire in the first-person drama. If Freud had fulfilled this promise, as Politzer had wished, Politzer would have had a perfect weapon against his opponents in classical psychology whose tilt was towards introspection. However, in Politzer's view, Freud failed by not keeping dream acts at the level of subjectivity. Instead, Freud resorted to an abstract psychology which functioned mechanically. This mechanistic psychology was propelled by impersonal factors, psychical forces, psychical agencies that could not reconstitute the dream or the dream phenomenon in its concreteness.

POLITZER'S TECHNIQUE IN CRITIQUING FREUD

Politzer's strategy is akin to that of a Trojan horse. He begins
as if Freud and he are in agreement against introspection until Freud,
too, becomes an enemy whose crime of abstraction admixed with
realism and formalism is ultimately exposed. As allies against
introspection, Politzer points out that Freud's approach to the problem
of the dream promises not to end in abstraction. Initially he sees
Freud at this point as one who does not wish to take the dream
from the subject that dreams the dream. The dream is thus not a
conception of the third person. It is not situated in an empty space
without a subject. The subject of the dream is thus the one who
defines the dream as a psychological fact, the psychological fact
that realizes a desire.

Politzer, thus, applauds Freud for reattaching the dream to the
subject that dreams it and for considering the "I" as inseparable
from the dream, the dream that is a modulation of the "I." The
"I" is everywhere. It is in the dream act as much as it is in neuroses
or parapraxes. Since the "I" is ubiquitous, psychoanalysis will search
everywhere to comprehend psychological facts as function of the
subject. Therein lies the fundamental inspiration Politzer draws from
psychoanalysis. What is this inspiration that Politzer draws from
psychoanalysis? Politzer explains that the most evident character
of psychological facts is "in the first person," so that the lamp that
lights a desk is an "objective" fact precisely because the lamp is
"in the third person." The lamp is not "I" but "it," and to the extent
that it is the "I" who understands its being, that lamp is a psychological fact. Therefore, according to the nature of the psychological act in question, the lamp is either a physical fact or a
psychological fact. It would be a psychological fact only to the extent
that it belongs to the "I," which will in turn inspire the form that
the subject gives to it. In Politzer's view, the lamp needs to have
a special form when it is a psychological fact, the same as it has
a particular form when it is a physical fact. As psychological fact,
the lamp must undergo a transformation. As with physics, psychology
needs to have the psychological facts under study submitted to an
appropriate transformation that is consistent with its viewpoint. Only
this transformation can endow the facts with this originality. It is
the contextual transformation of the psychological fact by the

subject that provides psychoanalysis with a new definition of psychological fact. In this transformation, dreaming may be connected with concrete individual experience.

FREUD'S FORMULA FOR EXPRESSING THE CONCRETE CHARACTER OF THE DREAM

Freud's formula has several facets to it. First and foremost it connects the dream to concrete individual experiences. The dream is the realization of a desire; an accomplished fact. This desire can be personified and thus transformed into Desire. This transformation is like Scherner's personification of the fall of concepts into the plastic representation that turns imagination to Imagination. For Desire to be realized we would then elaborate a symbolism of desire where imagination must catch up with concrete thoughts. There is a similarity here between the reification of desire in Freud's metapsychology of dreaming and Scherner's personification into Imagination. The similarity, however, is only in structure, not in function. Where Imagination in Scherner's psychology is in the service of desire, Scherner's desire could not be connected to the concrete individual. Scherner's is concerned with the generation of one general function to another. Politzer's Freud is different. Realization of the Desire in Freud is toward a particular desire. This Desire is determined in its form by the particular experience of a particular individual.

Freud's formula of connecting the dream to concrete individual experiences is one thing. There is, however, an extension to this. The dream thought is a concrete desire not only in terms of individual contents but also by the fact that the dream thought is a psychologically real fact. In short, the "I" stays in the dream. There is yet another comparison between Scherner and Freud. The theory of the former goes beyond the openly abstract theories of the dream and approaches the concrete in a way that sees in the dream a revelation that leads to the intimacy of psychological facts in general. Freud's, too, deals with the intimacy of psychological facts, except that desire of a particular individual is both the content and the motive of the dream, as in the "Irma dream" in Freud's *Interpretation of Dreams* (1990). There the content of the dream, according to

Freud's formula, is "a wrong diagnosis" but in terms of motive, Freud's desire is to be spared from blame for Irma's prolonged illness. Politzer would rather see the issue differently. According to his concrete psychology, the fundamental notion of this psychology must be personal and can only be the notion of the act. This act is the only notion that is inseparable from the "I," and concrete psychology can recognize the act as real psychological fact. Politzer would agree with Freud in seeing the dream as a psychical act that realizes a dream, infantile wishes or whatever. But Politzer would not be content until we see in the psychical act a particular dream author's own dream act, which can be explained by the latent meaning of the dream.

FURTHER ELABORATION OF POLITZER'S PROTEST AND DEPARTURE FROM FREUD

There is no problem between Freud and Politzer as to the mode of operation of, say, the mechanism of repression. Yes, an analysand may obliterate from consciousness an uneasy experience. But Politzer parts company with Freud and psychology in general if they attribute forgetfulness to general causes instead of to the precise fact that made repression possible at a particular time in a particular context. Freud's metapsychology is a psychology of general factors, like censorship, or repression, and the explanation Freud gives for each case claims precisely to explain from the point of view of generality. For Politzer, Freud's generality comes perilously close to introspection:

> Elle ne saurait donc répondre aux questions de la psychologie concrète, car pour cela il faut considérer les circonstances particulières de l'oubli, ce que le mot oublié signifie pour moi; il faudrait, en un mot, considérer cet oubli comme un segment de mon activité particulière, comme un acte qui, issu de moi, me caractèrise, il faudrait, en un mot, pénétrer le sens de cet oubli.

> It cannot answer the question of concrete psychology, because for that we must consider the particular circumstances of forgetfulness, what the forgotten word means to me; we must, in a word, consider this forgetfulness as a segment of my particular activity, as an act which, coming from me, characterizes me; we must, in a word, penetrate this sense of forgetfulness. (80, my translation)

We would only be able to penetrate this forgetfulness if we possessed the tools to do so. The tool for coming to grips with the meaning this forgetfulness has for a particular person cannot be introspection. That tool can only be a *story*.

THE POETICS OF THE POLITZERIAN "STORY"

Politzer insists that if we are to come to grips successfully with psychological acts, we must replace introspection with a story. Why? Because a psychological fact is a segment of the life of a single individual, and it is not the content and form of a psychological act which are of interest to us but the very meaning of this particular act. The meaning can only be made available to us by the subject's own utterance in the form of a story. In the process, a series of shifting substitutions takes place when we follow Freud: from a concrete point view to an abstract point of view; from an objective point of view to a subjective intuition. In contrast, when we follow Politzer, we have a different story.

In Politzer's method we have two alternative narrative forms. And here, the psychological life of another person is given to us in the form of a *story* or a *vision*. It is given to us in the form of a *story* when it is expressed in language (in all its cognate meanings); it is given to us in the form of a *vision* when it is about gestures or, in general, action. Both story and vision have a practical and social function. Language corresponds to a *significative intention*, whereas actions correspond to an *active intention*. It is first under this *intentional* form that the story and the vision insert themselves in daily life. The story is taken for what it is; the significative intention corresponds to a comprehensive intention. As to vision, contemporary life equally corresponds to its overall plan of action. When a person speaks, contemporary life only sees the significative intention. When a person stretches his hand to get a pitcher of water, someone hands it to him. In the case where the person speaks, he is understood. In the case of the gesture, a "social reaction" answers the person's action. So, we have *two orders of existence*, according to Politzer, *one of language, the other of action*. These two orders of existence would be equivalent to *word representation* and *thing presentation*. But once again we meet a similarity that exists in structure but not in function. In Freud there would be no simultaneous translation from thing presentation to word representation in any automatic way. In Freud's clinical practice, a considerable amount of working through would have to occur before action to define one's needs could become transmuted into language to define one's needs. In the process impulse control would lessen, frustration tolerance would increase, more self knowledge would appear, and so on. The *conventional story* in Politzer, like Freud's *manifest content*, is a simultaneous translation of the story in terms of individual experience at the level of latent content.

Since it is the individual meaning of the terms of the story that interests Politzer, he suggests that we approach the dream as a text to be deciphered. The structure of the intimate signification (latent content) is exactly the same as the structure of conventional signification (manifest content). To find one amounts to discovering the other. But we need a context to structure our inquiry. For example, if there is intimate signification (latent contents), it is because the person has a private experience. To decipher that private experience we need to go through it only to the extent where the person will supply the appropriate materials that lead to the meaning. We need Freud's free association as the entree to the dreamer's private experience. But, once again, the similarity here is only superficial. Politzer's view is that Freud errs by abandoning the inspiration of his own method when he concentrates on the verbal formulas that constitute the story. Freud should not leave the teleological plan to fall into realism. Instead, Freud should limit himself to the ordinary interpretation of the language and not go beyond the meaning to penetrate the private experience. Why should Politzer take that position? Because in his view,

> Lorsque le psychanalyste demande donc au sujet de dire tout ce qui lui passe par la tête, sans critique et sans réticence, il ne lui demande rien d'autre que d'abandonner tous les montages conventionnels, de dépouiller toute technique et tout art, pour se laisser inspirer par sa dialectique secrète.

> When the psychoanalyst asks the subject to tell him everything that goes through his mind, without commentary and without reticence, he asks for nothing else but to abandon all conventional editing, to strip all technique and all art, to let himself be inspired by his secret dialectics (108, my translation).

But that does not mean that Politzer would accept a retreat to an introspective psychology that would disarticulate the *story* of the subject with abstraction or a kind of formalism that would permit an inward retection. Nor does it mean that Politzer is following psychological themes simply as a context for a meaning for which the psychoanalyst is in search.

An example of the Politzerian story would be appropriate here. He needs to be quoted extensively to give us further attempt to see the flow of his thinking:

> Prenons un exemple concret. Dans le rêve de l'injection faite à Irma, « Irma a mal à la gorge » signifie « je souhaite une erreur de diagnostic. » Or, il n'y a tout d'abord « explication » que sur le plan des significations, puisque nous sommes devant une explication de texte ou plutôt devant l'analyse d'une scène dramatique. Le désir de l'erreur de diagnostic explique alors le mal de gorge, comme le terme latin « pater » explique le terme français « père », ou plutôt comme la jalousie explique le geste d'Othello. Pour que la traduction puisse devenir une relation de cause à effet, il faut réaliser les deux contenus. Alors « mal de gorge » deviendra « image » et « erreur » de l' « image » sera traduit sur le plan « ontologique » en faisant de la première la cause et de la seconde l'effet.

> Let us give a concrete example. In the dream of the injection given to Irma, "Irma has a sore throat" means "Would that there were a diagnostic error." First, there is "explanation" at the level of meaning, since we are confronted by an explanation of text or rather the analysis of a dramatic scene. The desire for the error of diagnosis explains, then, the sore throat, as the Latin term "pater" explains the French term, "père" or rather as jealousy explains the gesture of Othello. For the translation to become a relation from cause to effect, we need to realize both contents. Then "the sore throat" will become "image" and "error of diagnostic" representation, and the fact that it is the meaning of the "representation" which orders the presence of the "image" will be translated at the "ontological" level thus making the former the "cause" and the latter the effect. (169, my translation)

Politzer's critique of the proof of the dynamic unconscious essentially involves his comparison of manifest and latent contents. This comparison makes it possible, says Politzer, to verify that the latent content has been represented by an unforeseen sign which has another nature; the second story of the latent contents thus giving an adequate sign for the meaning of one or several elements in the dream.

Politzer's protest is that the descriptive must not be separated from the dynamic unconscious; that abstract location for lodging real and concrete sensations, thoughts, and feelings. The fact that these must now undergo transformation to reach the conscious mind means that the analysand is absolved of the responsibility of knowing and of confronting the original desire or the original lived reality. This transformation creates, in addition, explanations that can only be made in general terms. For example, Freud will follow the classical scheme of going from sensation to thought, a scheme whose reverse would make the dream the result of regression. If we have a Freudian scheme of progression and regression, we would then have topographical representations that have corresponding realities. This scenario, protests Politzer, is fertile ground for abstraction, an abstraction that is partly responsible for the analysand's acceptance of the real or concrete original desire. *The Freudian construction of the dynamic unconscious means that the truth is located deep down, and the analysand may only accept an admissable form of it.*

As Politzer sees it, no sooner had Freud discovered a psychological motive in an analysand than the human action behind the motive disappeared. The human act loses its precise meaning and drama in favor of a general one. The human act or drama has now become akin to some physiological movement or some form of excitation. We are now back to the functional formalism of the physiologist. All traces of humanity are lost. The term excitation would now possess Freud. He would forget more and more that his theory was only true to the extent that it participated in concrete human actions, precisely the act of the singular individual. He would, instead strive more and more to explain psychological mechanisms that for Politzer are empty.

The Politzerian story has many facets, in contrast, which include the following: 1) the first act of realism is the transformation of the significative story (latent content) into an ensemble of psychological realities; 2) the story is now immobilized and becomes the platform and the starting point for a second story. This feature of the Politzeran story potentially makes his inquiry a multithematic one, or at least a sequence of compelling themes that can fit into one coherent story. After all there are many kinds of stories. Stories come to us in the form of dramatic acts, in prose, etc. Some stories come from one-act plays, some from three acts, others in five. Politzer's strategy makes it possible for stories to come in one or more acts, so to speak. For him an essential premise is that we can call a psychological fact *conscious* when there is a realistic translation of the fact that the subject or analysand has made a determined story at the moment when the realization took place. Politzer recognizes, however, that not all meanings are available to a subject at all times.

The position that not all meanings are available to the subject at all times is based on his view of the *unconscious*, which says that "the unconscious essentially measures the gap between the facts and the postulate of the recitative thought" (191). A Politzerian concrete psychologist, therefore, accepts as psychological facts those segments of a particular individual's life that are capable of being submitted to a psychological analysis in a way that establishes the meaning of the psychological fact in the context of the life of the singular "I." This ensemble of the life of a particular "I" implies at each moment a translation of the immediate stories and the necessity to determine thematically the precise meaning or rendition of the act of the "I." Politzer's thinking here is very much like that of a mathematician undertaking the proof of a theory. What the mathematician does is to make the exception part of the rule so that the rule always works. For the mathematician, as long as those conditions obtain, the rule works. Politzer too makes the exception part of the rule. For example, that which cannot be translated from the dynamic unconscious into the perceptual conscious realm is simply not available and therefore not a part of the inquiry on psychological facts pertaining to the work of the subject to grasp his world.

For this reason Politzer chides psychoanalysis for developing a psychology of the unconscious that is rooted to the abstraction of classical introspective psychology. This old connection to abstract psychology is costly. Its price is to render psychoanalysis less empirical. Politzer's psychology, on the contrary, is meant to be empirical. The desire in the latent content is the same as that in the manifest content. There are conditions that fulfill the empiricism Politzer advocates. First, psychology must be a science that permits an adequate study of a group of acts a posteriori. Secondly, psychology as a science must be original in studying irreducible facts. Thirdly, this scientific psychology must be objective, that is to say, we must define psychological facts and methods in ways that are universally correct, accessible, and verifiable. The three criteria represent for Politzer the conditions of a positive psychology, which in his view, his concrete psychology is. His is a concrete psychology that represents a synthesis of objective psychology and subjective psychology. The human desire of the subject who tries to negotiate his personal need in a given context unites these two worlds, but the evidence for our interpretation must be concrete, objective, and not treated as material from a deeper level of consciousness, through a series of transformations, to the surface. It is the concrete desire or rather Desire in the dream thought that has primacy for Politzer. The dream thought is a dream act. It actualizes a desire for the subject who dreams the dream. The meaning of the dream is thus a determinate and unequivocal one that, once determined, must be a platform for determining the next and/or related story.

Politzer's critique of Freud's metapsychology, in a word, is based on his view that the latter departs from an original concrete orientation and erroneously becomes as abstract and as introspective as classical psychology. Politzer's unwavering concrete orientation is that of a phenomenologist, par excellence, who keeps the subject at the center of the observation of psychological facts. The subject has concrete desires that are actualized in the course of dream work, neurosis, parapraxis, etc. This subject, driven by desire and imagination, transforms the objects under observation in ways that alter both himself and his object. This immanence of meaning is what mediates the gap between the observer and the observed facts on the one hand and the postulates of recitative thought on the other. Sometimes desire in a dream thought will be available to be understood. At other times it will not be available. *It is part of the human condition that there will on occasion be gaps between facts and their otherwise unconscious or unavailable symbolic ideation.* For Politzer then, so be it until there can be a simultaneous and immediate translation between manifest and latent contents.

The Psychology of Georges Politzer

Amedeo Giorgi

For some strange reason, it has taken almost three-quarters of a century for an English version of Politzer's book, *Critique des Fondements de la Psychologie*, to appear. This inexplicable delay exists despite the fact that Politzer's works have been translated into almost every other Western language and despite the popularity of psychoanalysis in English-speaking countries. Perhaps the delay existed because Politzer was a Marxist, but that didn't prevent other Marxist sympathizers from being translated. Perhaps there was not interest because Politzer was critical of psychoanalysis, although he was far from being merely critical. Moreover, once the French took over psychoanalysis, they worked through the criticisms of Politzer and did not find his thought to be a deterrent. Indeed, almost all contemporary French psychoanalysts acknowledge the important contributions of Politzer to psychanalytic theory. In any case, English readers will now be able to evaluate for themselves whether or not Politzer's critique of psychoanalysis anticipated certain contemporary trends in psychoanalytic thought.

BIOGRAPHY[1]

Georges Politzer was born in Naryvarod in northern Hungary in 1903, but he left Hungary at the age of 17 because of persecutions against his family and settled in France. He studied philosophy and psychology in France and obtained his doctorate with a dissertation on Bergson that was published in 1929 and was entitled "Bergsonism: A Philosophical Mystification." This dissertation was essentially a critique of idealistic philosophy. Politzer was a committed Marxist-Leninist philosopher and, as much as anyone during that time, lived according to the principles of that system of thought. He also taught courses on dialectical materialism annually to workers at the Workers' University founded in Paris in 1932 by a small group of professors for the explicit purpose of teaching Marxist thought.

When the Nazis invaded France and occupied Paris, Politzer became one of the first and most consistent resistors to the occupation. He also emerged as one of the leading French spokesman for Communism and he edited and wrote many articles for the underground paper "L'Université Libre," the organ of resistance of French intellectuals. In February 1942, the Nazis rounded up about 140 French patriots, among whom was Politzer. He was given the choice between "reforming the values of French youth" as a collaborationist teacher, or of being shot. He chose the latter, with equanimity and peace, it is reported and was killed in May 1942, by a Nazi firing squad.

SOURCES

Most of Politzer's writings on psychology can today be found in essentially two sources: *Critique des Fondements de la Psychologie* first published in 1928 by Rieder and reissued in 1968 by Presses Universitaire de France, and *La Crise de la Psychologie Contemporaine*, which contains two lengthy articles by Politzer on "concrete psychology" written in 1928 and 1929, first published in book form in 1947 by Editions Sociales (edited by J. Kanapa) and reissued by the same publisher in 1973 as *Ecrits 2: Les Fondements de la Psychologie* (edited by J. Debouzy). *Ecrits 2* contains 8 briefer articles by Politzer on psychology in addition to the original two of the first edition. The first work, *Critique des Fondements de la Psychologie* is essentially a critique of psychoanalysis and was intended as merely the first of three or four volumes on the foundations of psychology. The others were to be critiques of Gestalt theory and behaviorism, respectively, and then, after working through the critique of the "newer psychologies," Politzer was going to write a full length book on "Concrete Psychology." The second work, as mentioned, contains shorter pieces on psychology especially psychoanalysis, as well as two lengthy articles on a critique of traditional psychology as well as Politzer's constructive alternative, "Concrete Psychology." These articles originally appeared in 1929 in a journal Politzer founded called *Revue de Psychologie Concrète*, the purpose of which was to overcome the crisis of psychology and to present articles demonstrating a unified concrete psychology, but only two issues of the journal ever appeared (February 1929 and July 1929). Politzer himself ceased publication because he felt that others were not so much listening to what he was saying about the meaning of concrete psychology as projecting their own meanings onto the term. He was afraid that the pages of his journal would simply be another instance of another movement being swallowed up by the establishment and so he simply gave up the idea.

Two other works in philosophy by Politzer are also available: *Ecrits I: La Philosophie et les Mythes* (Editions Sociales, 1973) containing 12 collected articles on philosophy, and *Principes Elementaires de Philosophie* (Editions Sociales, 1977), which is the publication of the course on Marxism that Politzer presented at the Workers' University.

POLITZER'S CRITIQUE OF TRADITIONAL PSYCHOLOGY

Politzer begins his critique of traditional psychology — and by this term he means the experimental psychology founded by Wundt and his successors — by observing that, at first blush, it may seem absurd that psychology needs a critique since rather than being dogmatic it seems to suffer from an excess of critiques. However, Politzer says that this state of affairs exists because no critique is truly penetrating and comprehensive, and in part, because there are always what he calls "conciliators" who keep trying to show that whatever point a critique is trying to make has somehow already been made by mainstream psychology. But, for Politzer, this is what keeps psychology stalemated because it only results in a change of form, but no real radical change. Politzer is seeking a change in the very foundations of psychology and nothing less than a radical break with all mainstream academic psychology would have sufficed.

For Politzer, traditional academic psychology is either out and out mythological or merely prescientific. A genuine positive science of psychology still had to be established and primarily what was lacking was conceptual and theoretical precision. Here's how Politzer came to that conclusion.

Psychology should be the study of individual human drama in the Greek sense of "doing and acting." For Politzer, drama means purely and simply "human action." No romantic, sentimental, or theatrical connotations are to be placed on the term *drama*. Instead of studying drama, however, because of what Politzer calls "The Metaphysics of the Soul" — which was rooted in philosophy and theology prior to psychology's independence as a discipline — mythical entities that are beyond the interest of psychology, such as mental processes, spiritual facts, phenomena of consciousness, mental faculties, etc., were substituted for human reality. Politzer calls this the "animistic tradition" and says that there is no way to save it. One can only ignore it and start again.

In effect, for Politzer, traditional psychology creates a second nature that is constituted like the first and is composed of processes and phenomena that are parallel to physical nature but somehow simultaneously *sui generis*. In the words of Politzer:

> We find, in other words, that psychology places a second nature in parallel with nature, constituted like the first by phenomena and processes, but *sui generis*. To the study of physical reality, insofar as it is a reality, corresponds the study of a reality *sui generis* "insofar as it is such", to the phenomenology of nature corresponds the phenomenology of the soul, to the physics of the phenomena of nature there corresponds the physics of representations. And as in modern physics, modern psychology also began with mechanism only to orient itself later toward dynamism. Next to physics we thus find a second physics.
>
> This second physics substitutes for the multiplicity of individual, singular human beings who play out drama, the unique universe of spiritual processes, just as physics substituted for the multiplicity of gods, nymphs, and fawns, the unique universe of matter. Instead of the way in which drama is carved out from the multiplicity of individual persons and dramatic events, psychology has substituted the great manifestations of spiritual nature: perception, memory, will, intelligence, the study of which it pursues in the same way as physics is dedicated to the study of the great manifestations of nature: movement, heat, light, electricity.[2] (1973, 86–87)

This is what Politzer calls the "mythology of the real," which is created by psychologists by a number of transpositions of human drama, the only genuine reality, into this second nature, which he calls the "universe of the soul and its phenomena." However, the constitution of this second nature in no way represents human drama. It is pure and simply a myth.

The constitution of this *mythical reality* — this realm of spiritual processes — is what Politzer means by *realism*. Realism, in turn, implies *abstraction* because it replaces the history of persons with the history of autonomous and impersonal processes — or briefly, it transforms meanings into processes. Politzer (1973, 94–95) writes:

> We say that a psychology which replaces the history of persons with the history of things; which suppresses man and erects in his place an actor of processes, which departs from the dramatic multiplicity of individuals and replaces them by the impersonal multiplicity of phenomena is an abstract psychology.

However, abstraction implies formalism because ". . . dramatic experience relates entirely to the human level and to the individual in which life unfolds, (whereas) a discipline that is realistic and abstract can only study 'psychical phenomena' and one studies them as one studies phenomena in general" (95), i.e., by class concepts and generalizations. Again Politzer emphasizes that ". . . all psychology that works at a level inspired by traditional class concepts and poses problems with the aid of such notions is a formal psychology" (95). Each assumption betrays concrete human drama and in a specific way: realism denies the reality of the dramatic fact as it is concretely given; abstraction substitutes for the concrete individual, the proper subject of drama, impersonal processes, and formalism eliminates the precise manner in which dramatic facts are concretized to retain only a form in which all individual determination is removed.

Politzer addresses this critique primarily against introspective psychology but he also saw residues of the same defect in psychoanalysis, gestalt theory and behaviorism, the three new movements within psychology that surfaced during the early part of the twentieth century. Each movement initially showed some promise, but each also was not able to extricate itself fully from mythical or prescientific aspects of the old psychology because, ultimately, none was consistently radical.

Politzer was especially optimistic with respect to psychoanalysis because he believed that it was oriented toward the concrete human individual in a way that was "clear, sincere and useful to psychology." As opposed to the previous psychology, whose analysis of impersonal processes could never lead back to the existing subject, psychoanalysis at least dealt with the concrete individual and rather than assuming that psychological reality is simply "given" in perception, psychoanalysis understood that psychology demanded an interpretive method. Ultimately, Freud did not follow his best inspirations and, according to Politzer, in explaining his findings Freud was too influenced by his times and lapsed into realistic, formal, and abstract modes of presentation.

Politzer had similar attitudes towards Gestalt theory and behaviorism. Both began in a most promising way but then succumbed to the pressure of the old psychology. Gestalt theory was especially valuable in its critique of introspective psychology because it clearly showed the falsity of an analysis that breaks the unity of human action into elements and tries to reconstruct a totality, which implies meaning and form, from elements that are both meaningless and formless. On the other hand, Politzer believed that Gestalt theory itself still engaged in impersonal theoretical constructions and did not seem to be able to completely free itself from issues formulated by traditional psychology.

Behaviorism's virtue was the recognition of the fact that traditional psychology lacked genuine objectivity, which regardless of its final interpretation, was at least a concrete psychological fact. But behaviorism in its actual development became sterile because it fell back into physiology, biology or even a disguised introspective psychology, instead of simply ignoring traditional psychology and going about its own work guided by its most original idea. However, we should remember that these are merely brief comments reflecting Politzer's attitude toward these latter two new psychologies because he never did get to write the full–fledged critiques of them he had intended. He did say that they both had to be reformed in the light of his vision of concrete psychology.

But as we said above, existing psychology for Politzer was not only mythical, but also prescientific. What did he mean by that term? As we have already implied, for Politzer the only realities are physical nature and human drama. When psychologists transform drama into a nature of "psychical events" parallel to physical nature yet treated as though they were things of the first nature, they create a mythology and that has been a large part of the history of psychology for Politzer. However, psychology has also been prescientific in its handling of drama even when it has stumbled across it. Politzer lists three ways that traditional psychology has been prescientific: 1) it bases its analyses not so much on the effective facts of drama as on the faith of a tradition and thus proceeds by concepts and definitions and such a process is endless. 2) Its research program is erratic because a good criterion for achievement is lacking. Very often psychologists don't know whether they have the whole of a phenomenon or only part of one. We all are aware of how often in psychological research genuine solutions are not reached; rather we get tired of working in certain problems and then turn to new interests. This is what Politzer was referring to by this critique. 3) Research in psychology is truncated because it stops before achieving what was sought with the precision needed. Traditional psychology goes both too far and not far enough. It goes too far with respect to the details of experimentation in terms of apparatus, procedures, controls, etc., but not far enough with respect to the manner in which the experiments are conceived. The experiments stop before the level of human drama is reached.

However, if psychology has missed studying human drama, the latter has not been entirely neglected in human history because there is also the tradition of what Politzer calls *Menscherkenntnis* or "practical wisdom." He refers here to literature, theater, arts, and everyday wisdom. For Politzer these efforts do at least deal with human drama, but they deal with it prescientifically. They are prescientific because 1) they use unorganized procedures, 2) because there is usually an insufficient analysis of human drama, and 3) the findings from this tradition are neither necessarily rational nor systematized. Thus one rarely finds in this tradition more than conventionally determined meanings because effective observations are confused with the moral, social, and religious perspectives of the times. For Politzer, psychoanalysis has already taught us that we must go beyond merely conventional meanings.

Thus, for Politzer there are two false forms of psychology: *prescientific psychology* and *metapsychology*. The former stops short of reaching its target and the latter shoots beyond its target, and hence both are forms that are outside the interests of a genuine psychology. Literature, theater, etc., deal with human drama, but prescientifically and the best of traditional psychology was still prescientific for the reasons mentioned above. In brief, we have either scientism or literature, but not science. However, the worst of traditional psychology was metapsychological because through the processes of realism, abstraction, and formalism it transformed human drama into an alleged realm of psychological processes, which for Politzer, do not exist as such and thus really form a myth. How then are we to approach human drama and institute a genuine psychology? According to Politzer, only by returning to the concrete.

POLITZER'S IDEAS CONCERNING A CONCRETE PSYCHOLOGY

Concrete psychology deals only with human drama and since, for Politzer, human drama is one of the two basic realities, he is not guilty of realism, which is the making of a reality where there is none. Similarly, since he only considers the actions of individual concrete subjects he is guilty of neither abstraction nor formalism. Thus he does not lapse into metapsychology. Moreover, since science is for Politzer, the organized systematic knowledge of effective reality, he feels that he is at the threshold of a proper scientific activity rather than remaining at a prescientific level. He admits that his science does not exist yet. But he also claims that he is past being stuck at merely a prescientific level.

To deal with human drama is to say something about someone. Human drama is a singular event taking place in space and time relating to a particular individual. The psychological fact is a segment of drama of a particular individual. More properly speaking, Politzer says that the proper object of psychology is the ensemble of singular events that unfold between birth and death. However, as implied, it is also possible to deal with a limited segment of these events — just so they pertain to the individual's drama. It also distinguishes between free and standardized events. The former appear during the course of the unfolding of an individual's life. The latter are attained by individuals in relation to physical, social or economic necessities. Thus, a general psychology dealing with concrete individuals is possible, but it comes at the end of research not at its beginning.

Politzer is also descriptive in his approach and he gives it theoretical status as well. One of the reasons that a genuine scientific psychology had difficulties getting started, in his view, is that realistic assumptions had led psychologists to believe that the psychological fact was a simple given relating to perceptual reality. Introspective psychologists thought it could be achieved by internal perception and objective psychologists by means of external perception. For Politzer, internal perception leads us to metapsychology, beyond the psychological as such, and external perception is not yet psychological, it is prepsychological; only the material basis for psychology proper but not psychology as such. One can only arrive at the psychological by going beyond the distinction of inner and outer, and for Politzer, science for psychology should be based upon an act of knowledge of a structure higher than simple perception. It is based on perception complicated by understanding; the psychological fact is not a simple given, but is constructed. In other words, it is not the gesture as such but the gesture clarified by the subject's description that is the psychological fact and this definition coincides with human drama. The psychological fact is behavior that has a human sense. Only in this way can the criteria of objectivity and originality of psychology as a science be established and the history of psychology up until that time satisfied one or the other of the criteria, but not both. By making human drama psychology's subject matter, Politzer also put it in a class by itself; psychology is neither human science, which deals with larger structure of social reality, but not individuals, nor natural science, which deals with nature but not humans.

In Politzer's eyes, his concrete psychology could have overcome all the classical antitheses of traditional psychology. It transcends the distinction between subjective psychology and objective psychology; between natural scientific psychology and human scientific psychology; between elementistic psychology and holistic psychology; and between inductive and deductive psychology. This was the chief virtue that Politzer saw in concrete psychology; psychology finally would have overcome all of its obstacles. The reason that psychology had not become effective in the world was due to the fact that we had not yet eliminated the myth of a metapsychology and not to the fact that the paralysis of prescientific psychology. But of course, in terms of objective history, not only was concrete psychology another failure, it is almost wholly unknown except for occasional reminders, even in present day France. I am not sure it deserves the latter fate.

PSYCHOANALYSIS AS CONCRETE PSYCHOLOGY

Politzer listed three criteria for an adequate empirical science of psychology: (1) psychology must be an *a posteriori* science, i.e., the adequate study of a group of facts; (2) it must be original, i.e., study facts irreducible to other sciences and (3) it must be objective, i.e., define the psychological fact and method in such a way that they are in principle universally accessible and verifiable. Politzer's view was that all three conditions were never satisfied in the history of psychology. For example, introspectionism sacrificed the third condition (objectivity), and behaviorism sacrificed the second (originality). Psychoanalysis, he believed, could at least in principle meet all three conditions, but in fact did not. It could meet Politzer's first condition because psychoanalysis is intrinsically empirical. That is, one first has to live or experience difficulties in life before they can be cured. The second condition is met because Freud clearly argued, in opposition to the main trend of the times, that dream interpretation could not be reduced to physiological interpretation. Thus, dreams could be the basis of an original set of facts. Lastly, Freud's analysis was based upon a method that was, in principle, intersubjective and learnable, and the claim was that it led to objective, verifiable discoveries even though Freud was dealing with highly subjective phenomena.

Politzer's point is, then, that Freud, despite his self-interpretation, gives us a concrete, holistic, descriptive psychology that seeks the meaning of experience. This shows that Freud was not always formal, abstract, and realistic. But he was not always concrete and descriptive either. In effect, Politzer's critique is that Freud used concrete procedures and abstract explanations. The duality is in psychoanalysis itself and Politzer wanted to purge psychoanalysis of this duality. His bold claim is that psychoanalysis is not defined by the discovery of the unconscious but by its concrete attitude even though it practiced this concrete attitude with only partial effectiveness. Indeed, for Politzer, the unconscious is necessary only because Freud did not proceed within a consistently concrete attitude. I will review Politzer's reasoning on this issue and then show how Politzer reinterprets dream analysis without the unconscious.

POLITZER'S CRITIQUE OF THE FREUDIAN UNCONSCIOUS

For Politzer, the unconscious was necessary only to the extent that Freud yielded to the temptations to be formal, abstract, and realistic. Politzer points out that the *latent* unconscious is proven by Freud by appealing to dreams, memories and hypnotic states. In each case, the strategy is the same. The subject can describe the experience (dream, memory, etc.) but yet, the meaning of the experience escapes him. The analyst, by his method, thus is able to show both that the subject can describe more of the experience than he realized and the meaning of the experience can be expressed by the subject. Then the interpretation is made that the meaning was *in* the subject, but not in his consciousness. Since it had to be somewhere, it was placed in his unconscious. Politzer rightly observes that this proves the existence of an unconscious only if one accepts realistic postulates, i.e., only if one assumes that the meaning actually preexists the analysis, Politzer's interpretation is that the meaning is constituted later in the dialogue between the analyst and the subject. It does not necessarily have to preexist in the subject.

Politzer makes the same objection to Freud's exposition of the dynamic unconscious. Freud's justification of the dynamic unconscious is based upon repression and resistance. But Politzer says that these phenomena lead to a theory of the unconscious only by presupposing formalism and realism. According to Freud, one can see a certain subject resist certain thoughts during analysis and so they express themselves in a dream. Consequently, there must be a force that resists the entrance into consciousness of these thoughts and this process is beyond the subject's awareness so it cannot be contrived. Freud then concludes that the thoughts must be as real as the resistance. The proof, for Freud, is that analysis can overcome the resistance and disclose the thoughts. Therefore, Politzer says, the proof of the unconscious lies with the same assumptions that there are real thoughts present that are blocked by resistance (even though these thoughts are not experienced by the subject) and that these nonconscious thoughts can have conscious effects, and since real effects require a real cause, an unconscious as the place of such thoughts must be introduced. Realism and formalism are evident assumptions in this explanation because it is assumed that such thoughts really preexist the analysis (realism) and resistance is posited to be a constant general life force (formalism). If such presuppositions were not held, the positing of the unconscious would not be required.

Politzer reinterprets the whole dynamic process in terms of description of the events and their meaning and sticks closely to the facts. During analysis a subject describes certain difficult states and later he describes dreams. Politzer says the clarification of both sets of descriptive material (difficult states and dreams) would reveal the attitude of the subject toward these difficult phenomena. One would not have to leave the level of meaning because, with sufficient data, the meaning of an attitude can be grasped. But Freud, because of realism, posits actual images and representations as real psychic entities as part of the dream process. Politzer concludes his analysis by writing: "To say a subject has difficulty in admitting incestuous thoughts and to say he has resisted them is the difference between a 'human' finding based on drama and a psychological description implying realism and formalism." In brief, Politzer calls the unconscious the place of "invented descriptions." Rather, he says, all we need to assume to avoid the hypothesis of the unconscious is that a human being is not omniscient.

Since the unconscious is no longer necessary, how does Politzer describe dream interpretation? First of all, he gives Freud credit for introducing the distinction between the manifest and latent dream content. All other dream theories failed because they tried to deal exclusively with manifest content in a conventional way. But Politzer says that dreams are the result of a personal, deep nonconventional dialectic and thus cannot be understood in terms of socialized and conventional meanings. Secondly, he affirms Freud's emphasis that the dream is a positive phenomenon psychologically speaking. Most theories of dreams of Freud's time saw them as negative or as deprivations. Lastly, Freud differed from his contemporaries with respect to dream interpretations because he assumed they had a meaning that implied personal involvement whereas others mostly tried to understand them physiologically, biologically, or organically.

For Politzer, when Freud said that the dream is a fulfillment of a desire, he was describing a concrete psychological fact.

I shall now try to reconstruct the dream process and its explanation as Politzer views it and indicate as well just why Freud introduced the unconscious. We begin with the fact that the dreamer dreams a dream from the perspective of dreaming consciousness. The waking consciousness of the dreamer reports the dream via memory. This is the first description or what is called the manifest content in psychoanalysis. The first description is usually puzzling. In analysis, the dreamer is asked to free associate to this first description. This produces a second description or "latent content" also from the perspective of waking consciousness. What is the difference between the manifest and latent dream contents for Politzer? He says that there is really one content of the dream, the *latent content*, because only that description leads to an effective analysis of the meaning of the dream. The manifest content of the dream is a "scenic montage" that only partially and incompletely expresses the lived attitude of the subject that is its source. And since the meaning of the dream is made explicit only through description, one can honestly say that it is by means of description — the second description — that the being of the first person of the dreaming subject can be made known. Consequently, the latent content of the dream is a description, a narrative, the theme of which is precisely a lived attitude.

Now, Politzer continues, if analysis is necessary to bring out this more thorough description it is specifically because the first description, the manifest content, is not an exhaustive account of what has been lived through by the subject. Closely examined, the manifest content, as noted above, is really only a "scenic montage" or an unconventional expression of what has actually been lived. Indeed, the mystery of the dream is precisely the inadequacy of the first description vis-a-vis the veritable richness and complexity of the content of the attitude that constitutes it. Politzer writes: "Being in first person contains more than the available description shows" (1968, 189). Now, Freud, in positing the latent content, tries to make the difference between "being in the first person" and its description, disappear. In other words, the latent content is nothing other than the adequate description of the lived attitude, and in making the uncovering of the latent content a part of analysis, there is an implicit assumption that there will always be an adequate description for "first person being." For Politzer, this means that one is establishing the principle that one cannot live more than can be thought; that all behavior presupposes, ultimately, an adequate description. This is what Politzer calls the hidden assumption of "articulate thought" and it is what is behind the postulate of the conventionality of meaning that other theorists applied to the manifest content. That is, the assumption is that everything is exhaustively describable because it can be sufficiently articulated. It means that psychological analysis must of necessity be a complete analysis. That is why, says Politzer, that when a behavior or a lived attitude is more than the accompanying description, one can always project into an unconscious what is lacking in the actual description in order to make it adequate. This is the real function of the unconscious. It is the place where the "lacking description" can be found. But Politzer says that the motivation operating here is to save the postulate of "articulate thought," not to account for the facts as they appear.

Politzer draws out the intellectualistic or rationalistic prejudice of such an interpretation. It is the priority of representation over being; the primacy of the reflective attitude; it is the affirmation of knowledge over life. Politzer, himself, however, reverses the priority. Being exceeds knowledge: the human subject is not omniscient and not everything that escapes the subject is available to the analyst. The unconscious is not necessary and a concrete science recognizes this sort of limit.

The relation, then, of manifest content to latent content, is something like essence and example or genus and species. The metaphors that Politzer uses are: the latent content is to the manifest content what a theme is to a play; or what the idea of a wish is to an expression of its concrete fulfillment; or the way that the idea of jealousy explains the diverse behavior of Othello; or the way that the rules of tennis are present while players are playing a match. The dream has only one content, the latent content, which is the work of a first-person dialectic, and it has it immediately and not in disguise. The dream is a modulation of the subject who dreams. It is personally and intimately attached to the dreaming subject and expresses the secret dialectic of that subject.

Politzer is little known in English language circles, so I am not aware of any critiques of his position by English-speaking Freudian analysts. However, in France, two former Lacanians, Laplanche and

Leclaire (1966), while giving Politzer credit for his indepth study of psychoanalysis, have criticized him for his position vis-a-vis the unconscious. They want to retain a Freudian conception of the unconscious that is in principle inaccessible to the subject and they say that Politzer erred in two ways: 1) he leveled subjectivity by saying that the psychological fact had to relate to first person subjectivity. They would say that subjectivity is multilayered. 2) They say that Politzer makes the manifest content of the dream a text and the latent content a meaning and thus he can dismiss the unconscious. In their structuralist interpretation, even the latent content is a text that needs deciphering and thus there is room for a Freudian unconscious that springs from the depths of subjectivity.

Unfortunately, the Laplanche and Leclaire (1966) interpretation has become the standard interpretation of Politzer, but I think it is limited and biased in terms of linguistics. At the very conference in which they presented their paper, Merleau-Ponty (1966, 143) is summarized as saying:

> He does not think that the opposition between text and meaning, as has been maintained, can give an account of the major intention of Politzer. The latter (the intention) consists in rediscovering beyond "conventional language" a primordial symbolism of which the dream constitutes a sample. Only, this primordial symbolism is not to be sought properly speaking in language . . . but in a certain perceptual articulation, in a relation between the visible and the invisible that Merleau-Ponty designates by the name of "latency" . . . and is not to be called a being which hides behind appearances. . . . the opening to being is not linguistic: it's in perception that one sees the birthplace of the word.[3]

That's how Merleau-Ponty interprets Politzer. But Laplanche and Leclaire, by interpreting what Politzer says linguistically, tend to reduce him and thus find a way of preserving the Freudian understanding of the unconscious. Taking up Politzer's ideas within his own vision of concrete psychology might make his vision of Freudian psychoanalysis more powerful than Laplanche and Leclaire allowed. In any case, the task Politzer envisioned still lies before us, and English readers will now have the opportunity to take it up.

Notes to Foreword

1. The information concerning the life of Politzer given in this section was taken from G. Congniot (1977) and J. Kanapa (1947).

2. All translations are by the author.

3. The conference at which these comments were made was held in 1960 in Bonneville, Belgium, and Merleau-Ponty died in 1961. The book was published in 1966, so others summarized his viewpoints.

References

Cogniot, G. (1977). Biographie de Georges Politzer. In G. Politzer, Principes élémentaires de philosophie, 1–8. Editions Sociales: Paris.

Kanapa, J. (1947). Préface. In G. Politzer, La crise de la psychologie contemporaine, 7–13. Éditions Sociales: Paris.

Politzer, G. (1973). Écrits 2: Les fondements de la psychologie (Éd., Jacques Debouzy) Paris: Éditions Sociales.

Politzer, G. (1968). Critiques des fondements de la psychologie. Paris: Presses Universitaire de France. (Original work published in 1928)

Laplanche, J. and Leclaire, S. (1966). L'inconscient: Une étude psychanalytique. In Ey, H. (Ed.), L'inconscient, 95–130. Paris: Desclee de Brouwer.

Merleau-Ponty, M. (1966). In Ey, H. (Ed.), L'inconscient, 143. Paris: Desclee de Brouwer.

CRITIQUE OF THE FOUNDATIONS OF PSYCHOLOGY

Georges Politzer

AUTHOR'S PREFACE

This work is not a formal introduction. We are not trying dogmatically to present the total entity of psychoanalysis nor one of its parts, but to reflect on it from our own point of view. Since our work assumes knowledge of psychoanalysis, we have left out all that is simply technical articulation or pure question of fact, when we saw in it nothing significant from our standpoint. This explains why certain aspects of psychoanalysis which, as with sexuality, should figure in foremost dogmatic statements, do not appear at all in this work.

We are not, on the other hand, in favor of that method that consists of justifying the "ifs" and "buts" with appropriate quotations. And if we have quoted less often than usual in works like this, it is because our exact interpretation can only be verified by personal reflection. We have relinquished, in the same way, the conception that inspires most French philosophical works, which consists of assuming the reader to be absolutely passive, not to say stupid, and to dispense him of any effort of personal reflection, we all but do the work for him.

This method is superficial and can only give a false clarity. Difficulty and obscurity, clarity and ease are not synonyms. If the preciseness of the idea is sufficient in itself, developments of it that help save the reader from making any effort are useless, especially since they are absolutely of no interest to the author himself.

That is why we have omitted nearly everything that is not the statement and development of the ideas themselves. After saying once as clearly as possible in what sense we reproach classical psychologists for treating psychological facts as "things," we have

1

consistently omitted comparing with Bergson's work the signification that this reproach has for us. We also know that we are far from being the only ones to use the term *concrete*, but the meaning this word has in our text must preclude all confusion, even though we did not review all its significations. In the same manner, we have not taken one by one the diverse definitions of the psychological fact and the classical critiques of introspection to show that the former all imply abstraction and the latter have left out the essential. And, in the same way, we have not elaborated on the idea of drama; we have not shown in each of Freud's theoretical constructions the way in which abstraction lets them be reproduced from a concrete fact and the manner in which this concrete fact can be rediscovered by reversing the path of abstraction. And we could quote still more instances where we avoided development.

All these developments would not have been useless. But the reader who is willing to make the necessary effort will know how to find them by himself, whereas for those who refuse to make such an effort, all the developments in the world would never be sufficient.

We, however, do not want to use this consideration to conceal what is vague and provisional in this study. Our work is a starting point, first because it is only volume 1 of the *Materiaux*, and, more to the point, because it is part of a series of preliminary writings. If we have not, for example, developed the idea of signification and the idea of drama to the point where their duality, a little bothersome in the present text, would have been replaced by a clear conception of their relationship, it is because the elements of this development are already part of volume 2 of the *Materiaux*, which will deal with Gestalt theory. It is for the same reason that, while using the idea of form, we have not elaborated on it. Other points, such as, for example, the analysis of the notion of consciousness or the systematic study of all these classical steps that we have shown along the way, can only be developed in the *Essai* (Essay) that will follow the *Materiaux*.

If we are lucky enough to meet some critics sufficiently enlightened not to give us again, under the pretext that we break down open doors, exactly what we want to talk about, it will perhaps become apparent that we could not, in doing this work, find many points of support — at least not in French psychological literature. We will then accept this easy idea that we want psychoanalysis exposed in terms of Gestalt theory and of behavior. But let us not forget then that our position vis-a-vis Gestalt theory and behaviorism will only be defined by the studies that we intend to devote to them.

In a general manner, the question of knowing to what extent the reflections contained in this volume or in the following ones are "original" does not interest us, and if we raise it, it is uniquely to clear up one more point. Some comparisons made will be legitimate, but we must not forget this: we must discuss the problems in such a way that the discussion, without going back toward that psychology that exists only for the historian, can begin again from a new base and then go on to a new level. That our formulas can be found elsewhere, or that they later are found inadequate, is not important, because for now it is not about formulas, but about a new orientation.

INTRODUCTION

1. If no one thinks of contesting the general affirmation that theories are mortal and that science can only advance on its own ruins, it is not possible to have its representatives ascertain the death of a present theory. The majority of scientists consists of researchers who, having neither a sense of life, nor of truth, can only work in the shadow of officially recognized principles: we cannot ask them to recognize a fact that is not "given," but that has to be created. For their historical role is quite different: it consists of the work of expansion and exploitation; it is through them that the "principles" spend their vital energy; respected instruments of science, they are incapable of renewing it and renewing themselves. And so they recognize the mortality of all theories, even theirs, but only in the abstract: that the moment of death has already arrived still seems incredible to them.

2. That is why psychologists are outraged when they are told of the death of official psychology, of this psychology that proposes to study *psychological processes*, either by wanting to grasp them in themselves, or in their physiological concomitants or determinants, or in the last resort with "mixed" methods.

It is not that psychology possesses fruitful and positive results that we could doubt only by denying the scientific spirit itself: we know that for the moment there are only "lost" researches, on one hand, and, on the other hand, promises, and that a lot is to be expected from a mysterious improvement that the future will generously bring. It is not even as if there is, at least with regard to what has already been done, a unanimous agreement among psychologists, an agreement that can discourage "fanatics" in advance: we know that the history of psychology in the past 50 years is just an epic of disillusion and that, even today, new programs are launched each day to focus hopes that are once again available.

If psychologists protest, and if they can protest with a certain appearance of good faith, it is because they have succeeded in taking refuge in a convenient position. Their scientific needs being satisfied by the handling of devices, even when without results, and by obtaining a few statistical averages that do not usually survive their publication, they proclaim that science is made of patience, and they reject all control and all critique using as an excuse that "metaphysics" has nothing to do with science.

3. This 50-year history, of which psychologists are so proud, is only the history of a "frog pond." Psychologists, unable to find the truth, wait for it every day, from anyone and from anywhere, but as they have no idea of what the truth is, they do not know how to recognize it or seize it: thus, they see it in anything and become the victims of all sorts of illusions.

Wundt appears first on the scene to advocate a psychology "without soul," and starts the migration of devices from physiology laboratories into those of psychologists. What pride and what joy! Psychologists have laboratories and they publish monographs . . . No more verbal disputes: "calculemus!" We invent farfetched logarithms, and Ribot has even calculated the number of brain cells to find out if they are capable of containing every idea possible. Scientific psychology has been born.

But in fact, how miserable: it is the most insipid formalism that has won a universal complacency and with the applause of all those who, of science, only know the common grounds of methodology. To be sure, in appearance, the psychologists in question helped psychology by fighting the eloquent outworn ideas of "rational psychology," but, in reality, they built a refuge where, sheltered from criticism, it still had a chance of survival.

Once we could measure to a thousandth of a second the associations, we started to feel some fatigue. The "conditional reflexes" came, fortunately, to revive the faith. What a discovery! And to the astonished psychologists, Bechtherev presented *Psychoreflexology*. But this movement fell asleep, too. Next, it would be aphasia renewing the disappointed hopes, then the physiological theory of emotions, and then glands with internal secretions, but the only result was a tension and an easing of a powerless desire, because it was visionary, and, at the same time, after each period of "objectivist" agitation, the vindictive monster of introspection reappeared.

4. Thus, the arrival of *experimental* psychology, far from representing a new triumph of the scientific spirit, was really a humiliation. For, instead of being renewed by it, and serving it, in fact, some of its life was borrowed for old traditions that no longer had any, and for which this operation was the last chance of survival. This is what explains the recognized fact today that all the "scientific" psychologies that came after Wundt are only disguises of classical psychology. Even the diversity of tendencies only represents the successive rebirths of this illusion that consists in believing that science can save scholasticism. For psychologists looked for this in every fact, physiological or biological, that they could lay their hands on. And that also explains the powerlessness of the scientific methods in the hands of psychologists.

5. As for the seriousness of the scientific method, there exists a veritable hierarchy of scholarly conceptions. The world of quantity being the mathematicians' own world, they move in it with natural ease, and they are the only ones who do not display their rigor on a parade. The use physicians make of mathematics has already been felt sometimes due to the fact that it represents only a rented costume; the pure span of mathematicians is inaccessible to them and they are often narrowminded. But all this is nothing in comparison to what is going on at the next level below. Physiologists are very much into the magic of numbers, and their enthusiasm for the quantitative form of laws is often the adoration of the fetish. This awkwardness, however, cannot make us forget the fundamental seriousness that it covers. As for psychologists, they receive mathematics third-hand: they get it from physiologists, who got it from physicians, who get it from mathematicians. Thus, at each stage, the level of the scientific spirit drops, and when, at the end, mathematics gets to psychologists, it is "a little brass and glass" that they take for "gold and diamonds." And it is the same for the experimental method. It is the physician who has a serious view of it; he does not play with it, and it is uniquely in his hands that it always remains a rational technique without ever degenerating into magic. The physiologist already has a strong tendency to magic: with him the experimental method often degenerates into experi-

mental "display." What about the psychologist? With him everything is "display." In spite of all his protests against philosophy, he sees science only through the common grounds that philosophy has taught him. And as he was told that science is made of patience, that hypotheses were built on studies of detail, he thinks patience is a method in itself, and that it is enough to look blindly for details to attract the synthetic Messiah. He wallows among devices, throws himself into physiology, then into chemistry, biology; he accumulates statistical means and is convinced that, to acquire science, as to acquire faith, "one must become a half-wit."

We need to understand that *psychologists are scientists like evangelized wild tribes are Christian.*

6. Whether introspectionist or experimental, the radical negation of classical psychology found in Watson's behaviorism is an important discovery. It exactly signifies the condemnation of that feeling of believing in the magic of form without understanding that the scientific method requires a radical *reform of understanding.* Indeed, we cannot, no matter how sincere our intentions and our desire to be precise, transform Aristotle's physics into experimental physics. Its own nature refuses, and it would be entirely unwarranted to trust any future improvements based on an attempt of this kind.

7. The history of psychology in the last 50 years is not, as we are wont to assert at the beginning of psychology manuals, the history of an *organization,* but one of *dissolution.* And in 50 years the authentically official psychology of today will appear to us as do now the alchemy and the verbal fables of Aristotlelian physics. We will still smile about the resounding formulas with which the "scientific" psychologists began, and about the painful theories they developed; static schemes and dynamic schemes, and the theology of the brain will constitute an interesting study, like the old theory of temperaments — but afterwards all will be relegated to the history of unintelligible doctrines, and we will be amazed, as we are today by Scholastic philosophy, of their persistence.

We will then understand what now seems incredible, that the contemporary psychological movement is only the *dissolution of the myth of the double nature of man.*

The establishment of scientific psychology precisely supposes this dissolution. All the articulations that a notional elaboration has introduced in this primitive belief must be obliterated one by one, and the dissolution must proceed by stages, but by now it should already be finished. Its duration, however, was considerably prolonged by the possibility given to the dead theses to be renewed by means of the respect that surrounds scientific methods.

8. But at last the moment of the final liquidation of all this mythology has arrived. Today, the dissolution can no longer affect the form of life, and we can now recognize with certainty the end within the end. Indeed, psychology is now in the state where philosophy was at the time of the elaboration of the *Critique of Pure Reason*. Its sterility is evident, its constitutive steps are exposed, and while some confine themselves in a Scholasticism that despite the impressive appearance of its production is not advancing at all, others throw themselves into desperate solutions. A new idea can be perceived as well: we would like already to have lived this period of the history of psychology, but we constantly fall back into Scholastic fantasies. Something, then, is missing: *the clear recognition of the fact that classical psychology is nothing else but the notional elaboration of a myth.*

9. This recognition should not be a critique of the same kind as those that proliferate throughout psychological literature, and which show the failure of either subjective or objective psychology and that periodically advocate the return of the thesis to the antithesis and of the antithesis to the thesis. We cannot, consequently, start a controversy that can, once again, remain *inside* classical psychology, and whose only benefit is to make psychology spin in place. We need a renovating critique, one which, by going beyond the standstill where psychology is now found, through the total elimination of all that has been creates the obvious facts that must be communicated.

10. Contrary to all hope, this vision of the new psychology which the critique in question supposes does not emerge from the practice of the new psychology. The result of this exercise is entirely negative: it resulted, in fact, in behaviorism. Watson recognized that classical objective psychology is not objective in the true sense of the word, since he asserted, that after 50 years of scientific psychology it was time for psychology to become a positive science. Now behaviorism is at a standstill, or rather a greater misfortune has happened to it. The Behaviorists, at first charmed by the notion of *behavior,* finally realized that the following behaviorism, i.e.

Watson's, had no future, and missing the bubbling cauldron of introspective psychology, they returned, with the excuse of *non-physiological behaviorism*, to introspective notions, or else simply limited themselves to translating in terms of *behavior* the notions of classical psychology. We then state regrettably that, at least with some people, behaviorism served only to give a new form to the illusion of objectivity.[1] Behaviorism thus presents the following paradox: to assert it sincerely, we must not develop it, and to be able to develop it, we must not assert it sincerely, thus taking away its reason for being.

All this is not surprising. The truth of behaviorism is established by the recognition of the mythological character of classical psychology; and the notion of *behavior* is valid only when it is considered in its general scheme, prior to the interpretation that the Watsonsians and others give it. Fifty years of scientific psychology has simply resulted in the affirmation that scientific psychology is only beginning.

11. Classical objective psychology could not have had any other result. It has never been anything else but the impossible wish of introspective psychology to become a science of nature, and it only represents the tribute of the latter to the taste of the day. There was a time when philosophy, even metaphysics, wanted to become "experimental," but this was not taken seriously. Psychology managed to allay suspicion.

In fact, there has never been an objective psychology different from this psychology that we pretended to deny. Experimental psychologists never had new ideas of their own; they always used the old supply of *subjective* psychology. And each time we found out that a certain tendency fell victim to this illusion, we started from another direction thinking we could do better even though we started from the same principles. That is why these researchers to whom the scientific method was to give wings always found themselves behind in comparison to the introspectionist psychologists, for while the former were busy translating into "scientific" formulae the ideas of the latter, the introspectionists could do nothing else but recognize their illusions. And now experimental psychology is only beginning to recognize its own nullity, and introspectionist psychology is still at the stage of its marvelous and moving promises, whereas with psychologists who are not interested in the physiology of sensations, in classical laboratories and in the "emotional change" of consciousness, there appears the indication of a very productive direction, with a clear vision of its errors.

12. It is in the light of tendencies that are trying to separate from the influence of the problems and traditions of subjective as well as objective psychology, that the positive and negative aspects of the critique that we are undertaking must be defined. For, if it is understood that this critique is not to be the result of a purely notional work, it is not required, either, to start it from the bottom for it to be valid. It must strike at the trunk, the central ideology of classical psychology. We are not cutting off the branches but cutting down the tree. We are not condemning the whole, either; some facts will survive the death of classical psychology, but only the new psychology will give them their real signification.

13. What is really remarkable in the whole history of psychology is neither this oscillation around the two poles of objectivity and subjectivity, nor the lack of genius characterizing the manner in which psychologists use the scientific method, but the fact that classical psychology does not even represent the false form of a true science, for it is science itself that is radically false and all question of method notwithstanding. The comparison of psychology with Aristotle's physics is not accurate, for psychology is not even false in the same way, but it is false, as are the occult sciences of spiritualism and theosophy, which also affect a scientific form, are false.

The natural sciences that deal with man never exhaust what we can learn about him. The term *life* represents a *biological* fact, as does properly human life, *man's dramatic life*.[2]

This dramatic life presents all the characteristics that render a domain eligible for scientific study. And even if psychology did not exist, for the sake of this possibility it would have to be invented in the name of this possibility. The reflections on this dramatic life have succeeded in finding their place only in literature and theater, and although classical psychology asserts the necessity of studying "literary documents," it has never, in fact,[3] been truly put to use outside of the abstract aims of psychology. And so instead of transmitting to psychology the concrete theme it harbored, it is literature, instead, that underwent the influence of false psychology: writers felt obligated, in their naivete and ignorance, to take the "science" of the soul seriously.

Nevertheless, official psychology owes its birth to inspirations that are radically opposed to the ones which alone can justify its existence, and to make matters worse, it is nourished exclusively from these inspirations. It represents, in fact, to use crude terms, only a notional expansion of the general belief in demons; that is, the mythology of the soul, on one hand, and, on the other hand, the problem of perception as it is asked in terms of the old philosophy. When behaviorists assert that the hypothesis of inner life represents a leftover of animism, they have hit upon the true character of one of the tendencies whose merging gave birth to current psychology. This is a very informative history, but its narrative goes beyond the framework of the present study. On the whole, the mystic and "pedagogical" attitude facing the soul, the scatalogical myths, incorporated into Christianity, found themselves suddenly reduced to the level of a dogmatic study inspired by a barbarian realism, thus encountering the inspiration of the Aristotelian treatise of the soul. And while this study was to serve theology, it tried, also, to establish a content, by drawing indistinctly from the theory of knowledge, from logic and from mythology. Thus a web of themes and problems was formed, defined clearly enough to form an identifiable part of philosophy. We can say that right from its formation it was complete, and no psychological discovery worthy of this name has been made until nowadays: the psychological work since Gocklen, or, if we prefer, since Christian Wolff, was only *notional*, a work of expansion, of articulation, in a word, the rationalization of a myth, and finally its critique.

14. The Kantian critique of *rational psychology* should already have ruined psychology. It could have determined an orientation toward the concrete, toward the true psychology which, under the humiliating form of literature, was excluded from "science." But the *Critique* did not have this effect. To be sure, it eliminated the notion of the soul, but since the refutation of rational psychology was only an application of the general critique of things in themselves, the result for psychology seems to be an *empirical realism*, parallel to the one that imposes itself in science after the destruction of the thing in itself. And as current interpretation drops this extraordinarily productive idea of the priority of external experience over internal experience, retaining only the parallelism, the *Critique of Pure Reason* seems to sanction the hypothesis of inner life. The old stock of

psychology was survived, and upon it fell the nineteenth century in fashion: experience and calculation. That was the beginning of the deplorable story, the *Carmen Miserabile.*

15. The worship of the soul is essential for Christianity. The old theme of perception would never have been enough to produce psychology, for its strength comes from religion. The theology of the soul, once established in tradition, survived Christianity, and continues today feeding from the ordinary sustenance of all the scholastics. The respect with which it succeeded in surrounding itself, thanks to the scientific disguise, allowed it to vegetate a little longer, and it succeeded in surviving because of this disguise.

It would be wrong, then, to say that classical psychology only feeds on the past. It succeeded, instead, in joining some modern exigencies, and the inner life, in the "phenomenist" sense of the word, succeeded in becoming a "value."

The ideology of bourgeoisie would not have been complete if it had not found its own mystique. After several tries it seems now to have found it in the inner life of psychology. The inner life is perfectly suited to that destination. Its essence is that of our very civilization, that is, *abstraction*, for it only implies that life in general, and man in general, and the "wise men" of today are happy to inherit this aristocratic conception of man with a cluster of costly problems.

The religion of the inner life seems to be the best defense against the dangers of a real renovation. As it implies no linking to any determinate truth, but simply a disinterested game with forms and qualities, it gives the illusion of life and "spiritual" progress, whereas abstraction, being its essence, puts a stop to all real life; and as it is affected only by its own expansion, it is only an eternal pretext to ignore the truth.

That is why inner life is preached by all those who want to win over those desirous of improvement before they can attach themselves to their real object, so that their greed for qualities replaces their comprehension of truth. That is also why those who are too weak to show themselves as being "difficult" grasp the outstretched hand for this offer to be saved while contemplating their navel seems really irresistible. . . .

16. Classical psychology then is doubly false: false with regard to science and false with regard to the spirit. What fun it would have been to see ourselves stand alone with our condemnation of

inner life! And with what pleasure we would have been shown the "scientific bases" of false wisdom! All these "philosophies of consciousness," which play with notions borrowed from psychology, all these wisdoms which invite man to deepen, whereas in point of fact he should get out of his current form, could have continued, with great effect, to realize the affirmation of the legitimacy of their basic thought processes in psychology.

But, in fact, both condemnations concur. False wisdom will follow false science to its tomb: their destinies are linked and they will die together, because *abstraction dies*. It is the vision of concrete man that chases it out of both domains.

17. This agreement should not, however, be a reason for confusing the two condemnations. It is much more efficient to separate them and to isolate the condemnation of the abstraction by psychology first. But this condemnation appears in the most technical part of psychology, and it is made by authors who ignore all our requirements. This meeting, however, to be successful, is not an accident: truth works on all areas at a time, and its different flashes end up by merging into a unique truth.

Since we want to separate the two condemnations in question, theoretically, we also need to separate them materially. That is why we need to start by establishing the sense of dissolution of classical psychology while adhering to the study of tendencies which, at the same time as they complete the dissolution, announce the new psychology.

18. Three tendencies can be taken into account here: psychoanalysis, behaviorism, and Gestalt theory. The value of Gestalt theory is especially great for its critical point of view, it implies the negation of the basic thought processes of classical psychology that breaks down the forms of human actions so as then to try to reconstruct the totality of *meaning* and *form*, from shapeless elements without significance. The consequent behaviorism, Watson's, recognizes the failure of classical objective psychology, and brings, with the idea of behavior, whatever its final interpretation, a concrete definition of the psychological fact. But the most important of the three tendencies is unquestionably *psychoanalysis*. It gives us the truly clear vision of the errors of classical psychology, and shows us from this time forth the new psychology in life and in action.

But as with the truth, these three tendencies still contain the error under three different aspects and thus lead their followers along paths that once again move psychology away from its true direction.

Gestalt theory, in its broadest sense (including Spranger's definition), on one hand, like Spranger,[4] is devoted to theoretical constructions and on the other hand, cannot seem to be freed of preoccupations of classical psychology.

Behaviorism is sterile, or falls back into physiology, biology, and even introspection in a more or less disguised form, instead of forgetting everything to wait only for the surprises of experience.

As for psychoanalysis, it has become so overwhelmed by experience that, when at last consulted was bursting to speak, that it did not have time to notice that deep within its heart it was concealing the old psychology that it was mandated to eliminate, and, on the other hand, its strength feeds an unimportant romanticism and speculations that solve only obsolete problems.

Moreover, it is generally either implicitly, or with a certain timidity that most authors dare pronounce the condemnation of classical psychology. They seem to want to prepare the work of those who see safety in the conciliation of opposites, without realizing that here again there is only an illusion, since it is impossible to place side by side tendencies in which each of them raises the previous question about the other or the others.[5] As for those who, like Watson and his followers, dare pronounce the frank condemnation, their assertions about the falsehood of classical psychology and the reasons for this falsehood are so vaguely articulated that they could not even prevent their own authors from falling back into the condemned attitudes, and so their declarations are to a real critique of the foundations of psychology what the general reflections on the weakness of "human understanding" are to the *Critique of Pure Reason*.

19. The critique of psychology, to be efficient, must be blunt, and it should respect only what is really respectable: false considerations, the fear of being wrong by declaring what one thinks or what one's thought implies, only make the way much longer with no other benefit than confusion.

This timidity can be explained by the fact that it is very difficult for us to tear away from this psychology that kept us prisoners for so long. The schemes it gives us do not only seem indispensable in a practical way; they are, also, so deeply rooted in us that they reappear in the midst of our most sincere efforts to free ourselves of them, and then we can easily take this stubbornness with which they pursue us for insurmountable evidence. It is thus, for example, that the affirmation that states that inner life does not exist any more than animal spirits do, and that the notions which are borrowed from inner life are so scarce that it is even useless to translate them in terms of *behavior*, seems, at first, impossible to conceive.

But let's be careful: this is only the temptation peculiar to old evidences. The critique consists precisely in taking them apart piece by piece to expose their thought processes and the implicit postulate that they contain. That is why, under penalty of inefficiency, it cannot stop at general affirmations that only condemn without executing: the critique must go all the way to the execution.

There are, however, still problems. At each step, we will wonder if we have the right to get rid of a piece of evidence or a given problem. But we must never forget that, for now, our "sensibility" has been falsified, and that it is precisely in going on that we will acquire a true vision allowing us to recognize what should be salvaged, and we will see then to what extent the evidences which, at first, seem insurmountable are less so later.

20. To come back to those tendencies we were talking about, the teaching that they contain for psychology risk collapsing because of the nostalgia which calls its followers to return to it, and because a radical liquidation of classical psychology does not allow them to be free of it forever.

That is why, in order to bring out all the rigor and significance of this teaching, we are going to devote a study to each of the tendencies that we have mentioned. These will be preliminary studies that will prepare the critique by shedding light on the plan of its components and in bringing in essential elements; they will form the "Materials for the Critique of the Foundations of Psychology" [*Materiaux*].[6] The critique itself, in which the problem that we just talked about will be treated separately and systematically, will be in the "Critical Essay on the Foundations of Psychology" which will follow the *Materiaux*. This preparatory and consequently provisional, character of the *Materiaux* must never be forgotten; it still does not include the critique, but only represents the first rough tools that will help forge the instruments themselves.

21. This research that we undertake in the *Materiaux* cannot, of course, no more than any other, be carried out in a vacuum. We

do not pretend to examine the tendencies in question "naively" with no preconceived ideas. Affirmations of this kind can be sincere, but never true, because a true critique does not exist without a feeling of truth. The whole point is to know the source of this feeling.

As far as we are concerned, it is by reflecting on psychoanalysis that we have perceived true psychology. This could have been an accident, but it is not, because today only psychoanalysis can rightfully give a vision of true psychology, because it is already its unique incarnation. The *Materiaux* must therefore begin with the examination of psychoanalysis: by looking for the teaching that psychoanalysis entails for psychology, we will obtain exactitudes that will permit us to remember the essential in the examination of the other tendencies.

22. The first wave of protest that the appearance of psychoanalysis unleashed now seems to have leveled off, although it was recently seen reviving furiously in France, and the situation between classical psychology and psychoanalysis is now not as tense. This change of attitude, which we can interpret as a victory for psychoanalysis, only represents a change in tactics by psychologists. We realized that the first way of fighting psychoanalysis in the name of morality and propriety was to surrender the field to the psychoanalysts without a fight, and that it is much more tasteful, and also more efficient, to acquire by a proof of liberality — which consists in assigning Freud his place in psychology, in his treatment of the *unconscious* — the right to have the reserves about psychoanalysis that "science" demands. So, thanks to a certain number of assimilations, we have passed on to Freud all the contempt that we now have for certain tendencies, and we assert then that psychoanalysis is only a rebirth of the old associationist psychology; that it is entirely based on the psychology of the *Vorstellung*, etc.

23. As to its followers, in psychoanalysis they only see libido and unconscious. Freud is for them the Copernicus of psychology, because he is the Columbus of the unconscious, and psychoanalysis, according to them, far from reviving the intellectualist psychology, is instead connected to this great movement which became apparent starting in the nineteenth century and which stresses the importance of emotional life; psychoanalysis, with its theory of the libido, the primacy of desire over intellectual thought, and, in short, with the

theory of emotional unconscious, is indeed the crowning of this whole movement.

24. It is not hard to see that the picture, which has become classic, that its followers give psychoanalysis, goes exactly in the direction of the wishes of classical psychology by helping it to recover its balance after the shock received from psychoanalysis. For by attributing to Freud only the classic merits of Columbus and Copernicus, psychoanalysis simply becomes progress made within classical psychology, a simple reversing of the values of old psychology, but only a reversing of the hierarchical order of its values; a group of discoveries that the categories of official psychology can accept, provided it expands to fit in so much material. Indeed, what the discussion thus directed is questioning are theories and attitudes, and not the very existence of classical psychology.

In fact, it is not evolution that is taking place, but revolution, only a revolution a little more Copernican than we think: psychoanalysis, far from being an *enrichment* of classical psychology, is actually the demonstration of its *defeat*. It constitutes the first phase of breaking away from the traditional ideal of psychology, with its inspiring occupations and strengths; the first escape from the field of influence which has held it prisoner for centuries, the same as behaviorism is the premonition of the next break with its notions and fundamental conceptions.

25. If psychoanalysts are collaborating with their enemies in the canalization of the psychoanalytic revolution, it is because they have kept, deep down, a *fixation* on the ideal, on the categories, and on the terminology of classical psychology. It is, also, unquestionable that the theoretical framework of psychoanalysis is full of elements borrowed from the old psychology of the *Vorstellung*.

Nevertheless, the followers of classical psychology should not have exploited this argument. Because by confusing the essence with the appearance, they only draw attention to the incompatibility in psychoanalysis between fundamental inspiration and the theories in which it is embodied, and thus digging their own graves. Indeed, in the light of this fundamental inspiration the abstraction of classical psychology bursts forth, and then the true incompatibility appears not that between psychoanalysis and a certain form of classical psychology, but between psychoanalysis and classical psychology in general. Also, because of the very nature of this incompatibility, each step forward in the comprehension of the concrete orientation of psychoanalysis has for a counterpart the revelation of a constitutive step of classical psychology; thus, the way Freud expresses his discoveries in traditional language and outlines is only a special case that allows us to observe how psychology makes up its facts and theories.

In any case, it is not enough vaguely to reproach Freud of intellectualism or associationism: we need to reveal exactly those thought processes that justify this reproach. Only, then we will be forced to recognize in light of the true sense of psychoanalysis that these processes whose errors we celebrated with so much pride are, in reality, only the constitutive steps of psychology itself, and the reproach in question will be revealed as a particular case of this illusion that does not stop persecuting psychologists, and that consists in believing that we have changed our essence, when in fact we have only changed our dress. . . .

26. We want to look for the teaching that psychoanalysis brings to psychology by demonstrating the preceding affirmations. We will need then, on the one hand, to release psychoanalysis from the prejudices of followers and adversaries by seeking its *true inspiration*, and by constantly opposing this inspiration to the constitutive steps of classical psychology of which it implies the negation, and, on the other hand, to judge Freud's theoretical structures in the name of this inspiration, which will allow us, at the same time, to catch, redhanded, the classic thought processes. Thus, we will obtain not only a clear vision of that incompatibility that we just spoke of but also important indications of the psychology to come.

But as the analysis must be precise, and as it must grasp the way in which psychoanalysis is elaborated and built, we thought that the best thing to do would be to study the dream theory. Freud himself says: "Psychoanalysis rests on dream theory; the psychoanalytic theory of the dream represents the most complete part of this young science."[7] Besides, it is in the *Traumdeutung* that the best sense of psychoanalysis appears and that the constitutive steps are exposed with care and an extraordinary clarity.

Chapter One

Psychological Discoveries in Psychoanalysis and the Orientation Toward the Concrete

What characterizes a science is a certain wisdom concerning a specific area, and, thanks to this wisdom, a certain power over matters belonging to this area. There is no productive science in which we cannot find these two characters of wisdom and efficacy. Take a physician: he knows amazing mysteries and he will perform miracles that the most daring magician could not have imagined. Talk to a chemist: he will teach you things that will amaze you, and see him act; the most reknowned occultist will appear to be lacking in courage and in imagination. And even if nature does not interest you very much, the wisdom and the power of these men and women will amaze you.

Now take a psychologist. He will tell you of the pretensions of psychology. He will talk about the painful story of his science. You will learn that we managed to eliminate the notion of the soul, the theory of faculties. If you ask him what he does, he will talk about inner life. If you insist, you will learn about sensations, images, memories, the association of ideas, the will, consciousness, emotions and personality, and other notions of this kind. He will explain that images are not psychic atoms, but rather are *fluid* states; that the association of ideas, far from explaining everything, is only a state of low tension, that you do not cry because you are sad, but that you are sad because you cry. And if you listened carefully, he will teach you that your personality is a synthesis. You will, indeed, be enriched by a certain number of means of expression, but don't try to express the wish to "go deeper in knowledge about the human being," because to cure you of such romantic hopes, you will be sent to a laboratory of experimental psychology to get an idea of science "such as it should be." There, too, you will learn great things. We won't object to your reservations on the properly psychological interest of the physiology of sensations. But we will teach you instead that you associate fairly quickly, that there is a sport that consists in retaining random numbers and in using a pneumograph to get a graduate diploma. And if you ask again to get to know the human being, you will be piously told that science is made of patience, that with the progress of experimental technology and a synthetic genius like Newton.

You are right: the psychologist does not know anything and cannot do anything. He is the poor parent in the large family of the servants of science. He only feeds on hope and illusions: for others, matter is what counts; he, however, is satisfied with form, for, over and above all his miseries, he is still an aesthete.

Why the false considerations? Psychologists did nothing other than replace one kind of confabulation by another one, one model with another one, and that is all there is to it. Knowledge of the human being? But all this is relegated either to the area of false problems, or to the one of faraway hopes. I do not think that we can have any other interest in the central structure of psychology than the one that animates those studies in which the value lies quite simply in the fact that by advancing in learning, one follows with sympathy the fate of an idea or a notion. Besides, we can already realize this from the history of psychology. It does not tell us of any discovery: it is entirely made up of fluctuations of a notional work applied to an identical set of problems, and that is a very bad sign for a discipline with scientific claims. In the history of psychology we have only seen a change in the language used and in where the accent is placed on different questions. But confronted with a real human, the psychologist behaves like a complete ignoramus, and, curiously, his science does not help him when he finds himself with the object of his science, but only when he finds himself with his "colleagues." He is therefore in the same position as the scholastic physician: his science is only a science of discussion, of controversy.

The first thing that strikes us in psychoanalysis is that the psychologist can acquire through it real wisdom. Oh! I am only talking of professional knowledge, but I use the term wisdom to emphasize it that is the first time that psychology goes beyond the level of language to grasp something of the mystery contained in the object of its study. This is the first time the psychologist *knows*; it is the first time that he appears like a magician, if I dare use the term, since it means something essentially *positive*.

The physician has public prestige, for his efficient knowledge makes him look like the legitimate successor of the magician, who only appears beside him as a timid forerunner. And the psychoanalyst acquires public prestige for similar reasons. For he appears to be the legitimate successor of the dream interpreters, the readers of thought, and the seers, who all, compared to him, are mere comedians. And the possibility of seeing both the physician and the psychoanalyst as parallels, because of their prestige, marks, in the history of psychology, a step just as "positive" as the use of all the devices that went from the laboratories of physiology to those of psychologists.

With the physician, the practical efficiency of the psychoanalyst's *knowledge* reveals the fact that we are in the presence of real *discoveries*.

The discovery of the meaning of dreams is one of them, that is to say, the discovery of the concrete and individual meaning of dreams. The discovery of the Oedipus complex, so discredited by Freud's enemies, is another one. Confront the psychology of love as it results from Freudianism with everything that classical psychology, including Stendhal's, can teach you on this subject; do this comparison from the point of view of the possibility that both give you a concrete case to understand, and you will be amazed at the difference. I am not intentionally talking about the much-discussed therapeutic value of the treatment of psychoanalysis. I am only looking from the point of view of the knowledge that psychoanalysis can bring to psychology.

Indeed, the discoveries of psychoanalysis translate into scientific formulas a certain number of observations that we can find in the writers of any sort and of any time. But this is because official psychology, heir of the theology of the soul, on one hand, of certain old theories concerning perception, on the other hand, and later of philosophical psychology, coming from both at once, was entirely absorbed by purely notional works. And true psychology took refuge in literature and drama; it had to live in the shadow of official psychology, even outside of it, as experimental physics first had to live in the shadow of speculative, official physics. This, too, can be explained. The illusory character of purely notional works pursued on the old theme of the soul and perception had to be revealed; then the hope of finding the *philosophical touchstone* through modern chemistry had to be dissolved, that is to say, by applying scientific methods, the old psychology or its confabulations had to be transformed into positive science; and lastly, for the concrete, to be finally able to speak, the wearing away of certain values in their different incarnations was needed.

I

These are not just simple value judgments: by analyzing the contrast that we have just shown, we will be able to discover in classical psychology the necessity of ignorance, as the necessity of knowledge can be found in psychoanalysis. This is what we are going to show in the example of dreams.

Freud permitted himself the luxury of devoting the first chapter of the *Traumdeutung* to the historical account of the problem of dreams. He adds to the statement some critical remarks that will justify his intervention in the question, and it is easy to recognize in this chapter the voyage of a man who can see in the land of those who have not seen anything. Freud gives his critiques a modest aspect: all that he wants is to show that after all that has been said, there still are things to say about dreams, or rather that the essential has not been said, because until now the question has been treated too lightly. And also, by comparing the different works, he obtains the picture of difficulties that a theory of dreams must resolve.

The theory that Freud considers as the most characteristic, because it expresses the most widespread opinion, is the theory of partial awakening, after which the dream is, as Herbart has said (cited by Freud, 70),[1] "a partial blurry wakefulness and at the same time very abnormal." We find in Binz the physiological translation of this conception:

> This state [of rigidity, *Erstarrung*] dissipates little by little as morning approaches. The products of fatigue accumulated in the cerebral cells are decomposed or carried away by the circulatory current. Here and there some cellular masses wake up, while everything else around is still immobilized. And the *isolated work of these cellular groups* appears then in the midst of our muddled consciousness, and the effort of the parts of the brain which group and associate cannot complete it. That is why the pictures are strange, united by chance. They are linked to impressions of a recent past. As the number of waking cells grows, the senselessness of the dream diminishes. (Binz, cited by Freud, 71)

"We can rediscover," adds Freud, "the theory of the incomplete dream, or at least traces of this conception, with all the modern physiologists and philosophers."

This theory represents the antithesis of the Freudian conception. It makes of the dream something purely organic, and a purely *negative* phenomenon, a defect "which is even often," as Binz says, "a pathological process." For Freud, on the contrary, "the dream is a psychological fact in the real sense of the word." Thus, it is essentially Freud's attitude regarding this theory that we need to examine.

> Considering the dream as an organic fact betrays still another intention. As such, we take away from the dream its dignity as a psychological fact. We can have an idea of what the biologists think of the value of dreams by the very old comparison with the man who, ignoring the music, would let his fingers run over the keys of an instrument. According to this conception, the dream would be entirely devoid of sense; how could the fingers of this ignorant man produce a piece of music?

By this Freud means that we systematically consider the dream as an event that does not enter the series of regular psychological processes, and that we don't want to attribute the formation of the dream to any of these processes. The dream then appears not as a regular psychic formation, a *thought* in the real sense of the word, but as a phenomenon which, in spite of its regular periodicity, represents, by its structure, an exception. Classical theory, instead of yielding to the originality and complexity of the dream, and of looking for the processes that explain it, persists in considering it as a derogation to the rules of the normal psychological work, as a negative phenomenon, so to speak.

This vision of the insufficiency of organic theories is present everywhere in the *Traumdeutung*, and it is evident everywhere that Freud wants precisely to make good this defect of the classic theories by trying to show that the dream is a *positive* phenomenon, a regular psychological formation, because, far from owing its existence to a scattering of psychic functions, it is only explained by a group of regular and complex processes.

We can then think, and the formulas of the *Traumdeutung* often invite us to feel this way, that it is simply the dignity of psychological fact *in the classical sense of the term* that Freud demands for the dream; and when he tells us that the dream is a psychological fact in the real sense of the word, the dream is integrated into psychology without having consequences for the definition of psychological fact.

In fact, it is not so, and it should not be so. This will to refuse the dream the dignity of psychological fact, and especially the way the theory of partial awakening does this, is neither a simple awkwardness nor a natural consequence of the dialectics of physiological psychology. For physiological psychology works with the notions and steps of classical introspective psychology, and, if it hurries through the problem of the dream in such a simplistic way, it is because in the area of the dream the categories of the latter become unusable, and the theory criticized by Freud is, deep down, *only the translation in dogmatic language of the impossibility of approaching the problem of the dream from the point of view and the notions of classical psychology.* Binz's theory reveals the fact that if we define psychological fact according to classical psychology, and if we use the notions that it also uses, we cannot see in the dream a psychological fact in the real sense of the term.

It would be then amazing that Freud could say, on the one hand, that the dream is a psychological fact in the real sense of the term because its formation, far from being explained by a scattering of psychic functions, is due to a group of regular and complex processes, and comparable because of this to processes of thought in wakefulness, and that, on the other hand, the expression of *psychological fact* could keep its old significance.

In fact, the opposite occurs. Freud claims the dignity of psychological fact for the dream only because he succeeds in showing original but regular processes at its base. But he finds these processes only because he starts from the hypothesis according to which the dream has a meaning. It is then because of this hypothesis that the dream can be reinstated in its quality of psychological fact. This hypothesis, however, already represents a rupture with the point of view of classical psychology, because the latter is placed in a formal point of view and is not interested in the meaning.

The problem of the dream could not be resolved by classical psychology, because this can only happen by accepting the hypothesis of meaning. Freud starts precisely from this hypothesis and discovers that the dream is a psychological fact, because it has its *own mechanism*. But by his initial hypothesis he left classical psychology; and as this rupture has great consequences, the formula that we have so often cited, and which tries to represent, in a way, Freud's entering in the midst of classical psychology, in fact sanctions the rupture with the classical definition of the psychological fact. We see here a well-known phenomenon in the history of the sciences: a model of classic interpretation collides with an "anomaly" that is finally revealed as a very powerful "dialectic ferment," and ends up by breaking up the classic model to become the starting point of a new vision: the dream has given classical psychology the same resistance as electricity gave to the mechanism of the physicians of the nineteenth century, and as Michelson's experience has done for the theories of relativity, it will establish the starting point of a new vision of the universe of psychology. It is then evident, from this critique of organic theories, that we will find in the *Traumdeutung* a new definition of psychological fact, irreducible to the one classical theory had gotten us used to.

II

This new definition can be derived by comparing the way in which the problem of dreams is approached on the one hand, by the organic theory, and on the other by Freud.

The theory of partial awakening considers the elements of the dream from an abstract and formal point of view. In the formal point of view, because we do not pay any attention to the individuality of the dream given by the meaning, and we only consider its elements in that they bring about the notions of class with which psychologists work. We will then draw from the dream only the teachings concerning those classes, and we will talk about the images in the dream, about emotional states, etc., always from the point of view of the class, and if the content intervenes, *it is only to be classified in general*. We will say, for example, that the dream is rich in childhood memories; but psychologists, although they had established this fact, thought they could dispose of it by talking of the *hyperamnesia* of the dream. And in the abstract point of view, because the dream and its elements are considered *in themselves*, that is, as if the dream were a group of images projected on a screen. It is true that it is hypothetically a special screen, consisting of consciousness, or inner life, and a special projector, the brain; but the explanatory procedure has exactly the same structure as if we were explaining what happens on a cinematographic screen: we must explain a group of processes that, in the form in which they appear, represent *the complete phenomenon*, and we must explain them simply as processes, assuming mechanical causes.

We call this step as a whole *abstraction*. It starts by separating the dream from the subject of which it is the dream, and does not consider it as fact by the subject, but as a product of impersonal causes, it consists of applying to the psychological facts the attitude that we adopt for the explanation of objective facts in general, that is, the *third person* method. Abstraction eliminates the subject and assimilates the psychological facts to the objective facts, that is, to the facts in the third person.

The dream becomes thus a collection of *states in themselves*, a group of states in the third person. Not related to the actual subject who dreams it, the dream is, so to speak, suspended in space; it is a resonance that is born by chance and dies when its energy is exhausted. The explanation can no longer be properly psychological, and we will try to have done with models that do not relate at all to the act of the subject in the first person. This is the source of the comparisons with the kaleidoscope, and the metaphor of the instrument played at random.

What characterizes the way Freud approaches the problem of the dream, on the contrary, is that he does not use abstraction. He does not want to take away the dream from the subject who dreams it; he does not want to conceive it as a state in the third person, he does not want to put it into an empty space without a subject. It is by reattaching the dream to the subject that he wants to give it back its character as a psychological fact.

The postulate of the whole *Traumdeutung*, namely, that the dream is the realization of a desire,[2] the technique of interpretation that is precisely the art of reattaching the dream to the subject who dreams it,[3] the entire *Traumdeutung*, in fact, which is the development, the articulation, the demonstration and the systematization of the fundamental thesis, shows us that Freud considers as inseparable from the "I" the dream which, being in essence a "modulation" of this "I," reattaches to it intimately and expresses it.[4]

The procedure that we found at the base of organic theory is not peculiar to it; we can also find it in the so-called psychological theories of dreams. This is natural, since physiological psychology transposes classical introspective psychology.

When Dugas, for example, says that "the dream is psychological, emotional and mental anarchy; it is the game of functions left to themselves, and moving with no control and no purpose; in the dream, the mind is a spiritual robot" (cited by Freud, 51), we find here again the abstract point of view which consists of conceiving of the psychological facts as entities in themselves, in the real sense of the word; in realizing them outside the person of whom they are the manifestations. By placing himself outside the activity of the first person, it is natural that Dugas can only find functional automatism. This theory, which is a close reminder of the theory of partial awakening, is the most abstract of the psychological theories of dreams, but the abstraction can be found in all of them, at different degrees, but definitely perceptible.

Not only can abstraction be found in all the theories of dreams, even the psychological ones, but it is the fundamental procedure of classical psychology. This school of thought seeks processes that are, so to speak, *autonomous*, because they are described not in terms of the actions of the first person but in terms of mechanisms. Classical psychology works with notions that correspond to the psychological facts considered outside of their constitutive relationship with the first person and that later serve as the starting point for the attempts of mechanical explanations, where only models in the third person are used and where the first person never appears again.

The most representative theory of this abstraction is obviously the theory of the faculties of the soul. The first person is broken down into faculties, and the psychological facts are no longer the manifestations of the "I"; they come from independent faculties that are and can only be entities in the third person. But modern psychology, which claims to have gone beyond the theory of the faculties of the soul, is exactly in the same position. The frameworks that the theory of the faculties gave us were carefully conserved (except that instead of faculties we talk about "functions") and with them the fundamental procedure that is at their base. The notions currently in fashion — consciousness, tendencies, synthesis, "attitudes," etc. — are notions that break the continuity of the "I" just as much as the faculties of the soul, and give way in the same manner to the use of third person models. At the most we can say that some psychologists felt the necessity to go back to the "I" and to the first-person models, but they stopped at that "feeling" and let themselves be caught up by classical influences.

Besides, this desire to reattach the dream to the "I" is not peculiar, in psychoanalysis, to the theory of the dream. It is present everywhere, in all areas where psychoanalysis has been applied, as in the theory of neuroses and that of missed acts, to set aside the extra-medical applications. What psychoanalysis seeks everywhere is the comprehension of psychological facts in terms of the subject. It is therefore normal to see there the fundamental inspiration of psychoanalysis.

III

But what is the precise meaning of this inspiration? The most evident character of the psychological facts is that of being "in the first person." The lamp that lights up my desk is an objective fact, precisely because it is "in the third person," because it is not "I," but "it." On the other hand, to the extent that it is I who understands its being, the lamp is a psychological fact.

Thus, according to the nature of the act that posits it, the lamp is either a physical fact, or a psychological fact; it can therefore be the starting point of two categories of essentially different research, physics on the one hand, psychology on the other. In and of itself (if this made any sense), it belongs to neither one. What is more, belonging to one or the other cannot become effective by a simple *verbal affirmation*, because this belonging is what must inspire the way the lamp is conceived; it needs to create the special form required by the dialectics where it must enter in. Thus, the lamp will be for physics (or rather for mechanics) a *material system*, and the properly mechanical study of the lamp is only possible in this form. It is the same with psychology. The lamp will be a psychological fact only to the extent where it is its belonging to the "I" that will inspire the form given to it, and it must have a special form when being a psychological fact, just as it has a special form when being a physical fact. Just as with physics, psychology must submit the facts that it studies to an appropriate transformation, consistent with its *point of view*. It is this transformation alone that can give the facts this originality without which a *special* science has no reason for intervening.

This *transformation* has as a base, in physics, the position of the facts as being "in the third person"; that is, as a group of relations from terms to terms and entirely determining one from another: the search goes "from thing to thing," and that is all. A mechanistic explanation, for example, is entirely immanent in the very plan of the process considered, one thing determines another without residue, the next thing determines the subsequent one, and so on: we never leave this plan and all is resolved in the relations in the third person.

The very transformation to psychology would be the one that would consider all the facts this science can deal with in the "first person," but in such a way that for the whole being and for the whole signification of these facts, the hypothesis of the first person needs to be *constantly* indispensable. For it is the existence of the first person alone that logically explains the necessity of inserting in the series of sciences a "psychological" science, and if, like all the others, it can abandon, in the course of its evolution, the temporal motives that gave it birth, it cannot abandon this relation to the first person that alone gives the facts the necessary originality.

Between physics — *science of the third person* — and psychology — *science of the first person* — there is no room for a "third science" that would study the facts of the first person in the third person, and which, however, by stripping them of their originality, would want to remain as the special science that only the relation it precisely rejects can justify.

Psychology, then, would like to be this *third science*. It wants to consider psychological facts in the third person and it claims to be an entirely original science. Its *realism* allows it to accomplish this miracle. Considering the terminology in fashion, ordinary psychology draws much more than we would believe from the old spiritualism for which the originality of the spirit is, in a way, *chemical*, in the sense that the spirit, while not being a form of matter as with materialists, is posited by an act whose form is the same as that of the act that posits the matter, and the spirit behaves then like another kind of matter both are in the third person. This realism alone can make one understand that the theorists of localizations have neglected the most immediate and longest-known objections. It is impossible to understand otherwise the psychophysiological parallelism and the way we have used it, and, in general, all the dreams of physiological psychology. Lastly, it is still this realism that explains how easily psychologists have forgotten the constitutive relation of psychological facts.

For if the spirit is, in accordance with realism, an original type of matter, then psychology could be a kind of *paraphysics*, describing a special world, said to be spiritual, but parallel to the physical world and not requiring special procedures. Its specificity will be due to the *originality of perception* required by this realism, and we will be able to treat psychological facts as physical facts, because the originality of perception will be the fundamental affirmation that will legitimize all the procedures which, considered in themselves, are absurd. Such a method, however, has no scientific stability, for the initial affirmation concerning the originality of *psychological perception* frees psychologists of all worry, and the constitutive relation no longer shows in the concrete work; we create and we describe, in accordance with the method of the third person, realities and processes, and even though we only elaborate myths, the initial affirmation of perception *sui generis* is still reassuring. And since everything must go through "perception," psychology and physics meet in the same object. Classical psychology strives to be able to consider the same thing twice in the third person: it projects the outside into the inside, from which it tries later, but in vain, to make it get out; it divides the world to make of it first an illusion and then to try to make of this illusion a reality; it gets tired, in the end, of this "alchemy," declares that there are only false problems here, becomes modestly quiet or falls back on qualitative nuances and "acts of life," and, while professing a deep distaste for metaphysics, for 50 years it ran from one metaphysics to another, for as it is, it cannot ask a question without having a metaphysical problem immediately come up.

"One cannot swim twice in the same river," and it is impossible to apply twice to the same things the method of the third person, while hoping to obtain each time a different kind of reality. Either we must give up psychology, or we must abandon the method of the third person when we study psychological facts. For the latter cannot stand the application of models that make the first person disappear and cannot enter into any impersonal process, because to remove from the psychological fact the subject that implies it is to annihilate it as being *psychological*; and to conceive it in such a way that the model of the conception implies a rupture in the continuity of the "I" can only lead to mythology.

Classical psychology ignores these exigencies, and psychologists did not realize that to remove the "I" from the psychological facts is to annihilate them; and that therefore all theory founded on this step can only be a pure and simple fabrication.

It may be objected that we are breaking down open doors, since psychology considers the psychological facts exactly like manifestations of an individual consciousness. And there is some truth in this objection, because the very people who criticize classical psychology in a determined and strict manner reproach it precisely for withdrawing into the facts of individual consciousness. "Some authors," says Spranger,[5] "limit psychology strictly to the subject, that is, to the states and the processes belonging to an individual me . . . ," and he later reproaches classical psychology for maintaining the subject in this artificial isolation, instead of reattaching it "to the forms of the historical and social level of the spirit."[6]

But we have to agree. Spranger is perfectly right to make this reproach of psychology. But that is because he looks at things from a point of view very different from ours. He advocates a psychology that will study the different ways man gets involved in the multiple networks of "values," or, if we prefer, the resulting settings. What we have called abstraction will appear to Spranger in a special way. As abstraction consists in considering psychological facts as states *in themselves*, and as Spranger takes the point of view of *vital forms*, he will essentially notice the isolation vis-a-vis objective forms, and he will see in this isolation a consequence of the limitation of psychology to the individual. He did not notice that the limitation of psychology to the study of purely individual facts is only *verbal*.

In fact, once psychology has asserted that its domain is established by the events of the "me," it does not know what to do with this me and, in reality, it does not do anything with it. For, having become phenomenal following the ruin of rational psychology, it only studies the multiplicity of "phenomena." Hume, at least, was honest: he clearly stated that the me is only this multiplicity. But modern psychologists cannot seem to state clearly the fundamental consequences of their attitude, and they would like very much to give meaning to the me.

There are, in this respect, several themes. We can resort, for example, to the model of reflection. In this instance, the me is the cause of the facts of consciousness, at the same time as it is the subject of introspection: what looks and what is looked at. Most of the time the me is simply the locus of psychological facts in the beginning and their synthesis at the end. But in any case, the me still remains abstract. It is a simple cause, a pure *functional center*, on the one hand, and an eye, on the other, in the model of reflection; it is only a word for disguising the naive realism in the second hypothesis and a cluster of abstract functions in the third one.

Classical psychology therefore talks about the *me*, but it talks about the *me* on one side, and about psychological facts on the other. As long as it studies psychological facts, it treats them as if they were in the third person, and it later calls for the obligation to reattach them to a subject. But it is incapable of finding a relation that can accomplish this miracle. It then takes refuge in quality and keeps individuality only on the qualitative level: adherence of the psychological facts to the individual is manifested only in the qualitative irreducibility of the act in which they are being lived. Apart from this emphasis by quality, the psychological facts are treated as if they were facts in the third person.

They would not be thus if their adherence to the subject was at the base of the form in which we conceive them. And this could only be so if they were not considered in themselves, apart from the subject, but like the elements of a whole that cannot be conceived without the subject; that is, as the different aspects of the act of the "I."

Here someone can object that psychology knows our exigence

and that it clearly asserts that it is a question of images, emotion, memory, and, in general, functions, only temporarily; that we practice this fragmenting only for the needs of analysis, for, in reality, it is about parts of a whole, etc.

There is, however, between the affirmation of a thesis and the realization of the corresponding attitude, an abyss. The profession of faith in question only means that psychologists do not believe that the functions they describe can come true one by one, isolated from each other, but not that the analysis of a psychological fact from the point of view of functional formalism is not a true psychological analysis. Here, then, is precisely the question. The totality that psychologists are willing to admit in man is only a "functional" totality, a confusion of notions of class. Such a confusion, whatever the degree of its complexity, is not an act, and does not suppose a subject, but a simple functional center, for we cannot, with impersonal elements, constitute a personal fact like the act, and psychology remains, with its false totality, on the level of abstraction.

Let it not be said that there is fragmenting for the needs of analysis, because psychology borrows its notions of class it knows not exactly where, and gives its justificative explanations only because the concrete is starting to worry it. But in any case, it is not from simple analysis, but from abstraction and formalism that the fundamental notions of classical psychology result.

In short, the notions of psychology cannot be considered as the aspects of an individual act, because they do not belong on the same level as the "I." The adherence of psychological facts to the "I" will only appear by remaining on this level: *the psychological facts must be homogenous to the "I,"* they can only be the incarnations of the same form of the "I."

IV

It is immediately obvious that these considerations do not help us obtain the "formula" of psychology. The exigencies that we have just talked about are common to psychology and to the theory of knowledge, and, in general, to any analysis of the mind. For knowledge cannot be explained by models in the third person, either. That is why Kant could not accept Hume's association. For Hume's association, conceived in the image of Newton's universal attraction, is something blind, going "from thing to thing," and does not imply a subject. Kant, on the contrary, with his theory of synthesis perfectly satisfies the exigence of the first person and of homogeneity. For synthesis, as he understands it, is an act in the first person, and, in the last analysis, categories are only specifications of the transcendental insight that is the pure form of the act of the "I."

The "I" of Kant, however, while being a "subject," is the subject of objective and therefore universal thought; its discovery and its study not only do not require the concrete experience but even exclude it, because we are and must remain on the level of transcendental logic.

Now, psychology, if it has a reason for being, can only exist as an *empirical* science. It must therefore interpret the exigence of the first person and of homogeneity in a way that is appropriate to its level. Needing to be empirical, the "I" of psychology can only be the *particular individual*. Also, this "I" cannot be the subject of a transcendental act like insight, for we need a notion that is on the same level as the concrete individual and that is simply the act of the "I" of psychology. Thus, the act of the concrete individual is indeed *life*, but the singular life of the singular individual, in short, *life*, in the dramatic sense of the word.

This singularity must be defined, also, in a concrete manner, and not in the formal point of view. The individual is singular because his life is singular, and this life, in turn, is singular only by its content: its singularity then is not *qualitative*, but *dramatic*. The exigence of the homogeneity and of the first person will be respected if the notions of psychology remain on the level of this *drama*: the psychological facts will be the segments of the life of the particular individual.

Segments of the life of the particular individual, to express that which is above or beneath the drama is no longer a psychological fact "in the real sense of the word." The lightbulb is something from the lamp, but it is not the lamp itself, and the lamp being my main interest, the place where it sits, my desk, is also something of the lamp. But the lightbulb is "beneath" and the desk is "above" the lamp, and if it is the lamp I am interested in, I cannot break the unity of the object "lamp"; I must, instead, relate everything to this unity, without ever leaving its level. It is the same with psychology. It is "events" that the subject lives, and the term "event" means that it is about a whole subject. My son cries because he has to go to bed. That is the event. But there is for classical psychology only a lacrimal secretion consecutive to a representation thwarting a deep tendency. That is all that happened. We therefore left the level of the *human drama*, of which the author is the concrete individual, and we replaced it with an *abstract drama*. In the first instance, the individual is something essential; in the second one, the true players are impersonal, and the individual plays, at the most, the role of managing director. That is the true meaning of abstraction: classical psychology tries to replace the personal drama with an impersonal drama, the drama wherein the actor is a concrete individual *who is a reality*, with a drama where the players are *mythological creatures*: abstraction consists, in the last analysis, of admitting the *equivalence of these two dramas*, of asserting that the impersonal drama, the "real" one, explains the personal drama which is only "apparent." The ideal of classical psychology consists of the research of purely "notional" dramas.

On the contrary, psychology, which accepts the definition that we just stated, does not admit the substitution of the impersonal drama for the personal drama. The event, or act,[7] whichever we prefer, represents for it the term of the analysis, and it is by the personal that it tries to explain the personal. The psychologist will then have something of the dramatic critic: an act will always appear to him as a segment of the drama that only exists in and through the drama. His method will not be a method of *observation* pure and simple, but a method of *interpretation*.

It is not difficult to guess that it is precisely in this direction that psychoanalysis is going. It is the meaning of the dream that Freud seeks. He is not satisfied with just the abstract and formal study of its elements. He does not seek an abstract and impersonal script in which the actors are physiological excitations and the plot consists of their walk in the brain cells. And what he wants to reach by interpretation is not the abstract "me" of psychology, but the subject of individual life; that is, the support of a group of unique events, the actor, we can say, of the dramatic life and not the subject of introspection; in a word, *the me of daily life*. And this me does not intervene as "owner of his states of being" or as the cause of a general function, but as the agent of an act considered in its singular determination. Above all, we are not referring to a cause void of meaning and content, but to a subject qualified by events, and which is whole in each of these events. The dream is thus a segment of the life of the particular individual: it can only be explained by being related to the "I"; but to relate the dream to the "I" means then the determination of its meaning as being a moment in the unfolding of a group of events of which we call the totality a life, the life of the particular individual.

V

Psychoanalysis, therefore, contains a new definition of the psychological fact. We have brought this definition forward in a somewhat artificial manner, by first expressing it in its most general and abstract form. It was necessary to start this way so as on the one hand to make apparent all the precision and the importance of the definition in question, by distinguishing the two stages in the progress toward the concrete, and, on the other hand, to show that it is possible to reveal the falsehood of this fundamental procedure of classical psychology that is abstraction, independently of any question of doctrine.

Freud proceeds in a more empirical and less conscious manner. He does not undertake, and that is natural, a general analysis of the procedures of classical psychology, he simply points out the mistake of the theses that derive from them on the precise points where he sees them. And, in the same way, he does not point out the consequences of his attitude and is not even able to formulate in general terms the fundamental inspiration of his own doctrine. Thus he behaves as if he had defined the psychological fact as we just did: he is interested in psychological facts only to the extent to which they are individual acts, and meanwhile he remains convinced that psychoanalysis is revolutionary only as a contribution. Instead of prolonging the point of view of the interpretation until a new definition of psychological fact can come from it, he considers it in the *Traumdeutung* as a separate point of view, which is not *the* psychological point of view, and tries later, in the chapter entitled "The psychology of the processes of dreams," to translate from the "psychological" point of view the psychoanalytic facts in the language of classical psychology.[8]

But as we can judge that the way we characterized the fundamental inspiration of psychoanalysis is not convincing enough, we will try to verify our interpretation by showing in a concrete example that Freud's attitude corresponds perfectly to the description that we gave of it, and then that our interpretation allows one to understand the tenacity with which Freud asserts in the *Traumdeutung* that "the dream is the realization of a desire."

In discussing the nightmare, Freud establishes a parallel between the method of classic explanations and his own.

"A striking example," says Freud (575), "will show to what extent the 'blinders' of the medical mythology stop physicians from seeing the facts. It is an observation recounted by Debacker in his thesis on "Hallucinations and nocturnal terrors in children and adolescents" (1881, 66).

Freud quotes the observation, but we can simply compare the two explanations.

Here is Debacker's explanation: "This observation is remarkable from a great many points of view, and its analysis points out the following facts":

> 1. That the physiological work of puberty in a young boy with weak health brings on a state of great weakening and that the cerebral anemia can be considerable;
> 2. This cerebral anemia leads to a change of character to demonomaniacal hallucinations and to nocturnal terrors, and perhaps very intense diurnal ones;
> 3. This demonomania and these religious scruples obviously come from the religious environment of the child's youth;
> 4. All the phenomena disappeared through an extended stay in the country, exercise and the recovery of strength after puberty,
> 5. Can a predisposition for the cerebral state be attributed to heredity and the father's former case of syphilis? It will be interesting to see about it in the future.

Freud calls attention to the last remark of this work: "We include this observation in the framework of the apyretic deliriums of ination, because it is to the cerebral ischemia that we relate this particular state" (cf. 575–77).

Freud's explanation is quite different: "It is not hard to guess," he says (577):

> 1. That the child masturbated when he was very young, that he did not want to admit it and that he had been threatened of severe punishment (his admission: "I won't do it again"; his denial: "Albert has never done that");
> 2. That with the growth of puberty the temptation to masturbate reappeared;
> 3. That it provoked a repression and a struggle where the libido changed to anxiety; in a secondary fashion, this anxiety took the form of the punishments he had been threatened with long ago.

Whatever we think of the last explanation, what is striking is that the physician quoted by Freud resorts only to general causes, like cerebral anemia, inanition; that for him the particular form of the deliriums, those scenes in which the child dramatized his fright, has no importance; that he explains only the general scheme from the "devil's" scenario and only by a general cause, the religious environment; that as a result, he never descends to the individual level to understand the facts in their concrete particularity; and that, finally, he leaves no room for "secondary causes." Freud, on the contrary, does not leave the concrete and individual form of the symptom in question, with all its particular details, and only individual facts intervene in the explanation, borrowed from the experience of the subject in question. Therefore, he never leaves the level of the singular individual.

That the spirit of Freud's doctrine is the one we have shown is demonstrated by the most fundamental affirmation of the theory of dreams, namely, that "the dream is the realization of a desire." Amazing affirmation, indeed, for it appears at the beginning of the book when the reader, influenced by the chapter about the historical account of the problem of dreams, on one hand, and the parallel Freud establishes between the old "dream interpreters" and psychoanalysis, on the other, considers Freud as the one who maintains "in general" that dreams have meaning.

In fact, Freud's discovery has an entirely different signification, one that is important for an entirely different reason. He is not the first to assert that dreams have meaning. He talks about Scherner's attempt to expand the problem of the dream in this direction (cf. 76, sqq).

In 1861, "Scherner made the most original and most impressive attempt to explain the dream by a particular activity which could only be displayed during sleep" (77). This "particular activity" is due to the imagination that, during the dream, "frees itself from intelligence and dominates completely." The imagination, to construct the dream, draws "its materials from the memory of the day before, but the edifice it builds is entirely different from the productions of the day before" (77). "In the dream it does not have the language of concepts at its disposal; it must show what it means in a plastic." "It gives a plastic outer form to the facts of our inner life" (77). This plastic activity of the imagination does not consist in simply replacing an object by its image. It dramatizes the thought by outlining its silhouette" (88).

"Scherner believes that the elements that the artistic activity of the dream uses are mostly the organic excitations that are so obscure during the day" (88). The imagination of the dream plays with the organic excitations "an annoying game . . . representing the organs from which the excitation originates in symbolic forms" (88). The whole organism, for example, is represented by a house. But

> it does not stop there; it can, on the contrary, represent by series of houses only one organ, for example long streets will represent the intestinal excitation. Other times, parts of houses will really represent parts of the body. For example, in a migraine headache dream, the ceiling of a room (that we see covered with revolting spiders, similar to toads) will represent the head (78–79).

Faced with these texts, and especially by reading the comments of one of Scherner's followers, Volkelt, the well-known German philosopher (cf. 79, section 2), where a symbolism as advanced as Freud's appears, we can think that Freud borrowed much from him. But Scherner's thought is fundamentally falsified by abstraction. The dream has a meaning, to be sure. We can even see with Scherner too, though only in an implicit way, the distinction of the manifest content and the latent content, the one established by the nondeciphered story, the other by the deciphered story. But the meaning that the dream has for Scherner is a general one; its deciphering, given Scherner's symbolism, gives general latent content, and the interpretation reattaches the dream to the impersonal organic excitations. But for Freud, "it is our personality that appears in each of our dreams" (289). It is precisely to this concrete personality that the Freudian interpretation reattaches the dream. Freud cannot accept the explanation of Scherner, who shows "how the power of centralization, the spontaneous energy of the me are enervated in the dream; how, because of this decentralization, the knowledge, the sensibility, the will, the power of representation, are changed . . ." because in his explanation Scherner only asserts the thesis of the abstraction. Thus, Freud does not know what to do with this theory and with the symbolism deriving from it.

Scherner and Freud both assert that the dream has a signification, but one is a psychologist in the classical sense of the word, and quickly comes back to the abstract after only touching lightly on the concrete, whereas the other one inaugurates the conscious and decisive return to the concrete.

To sum up the essence of the dream Freud needs a formula that expresses the concrete character of the dream, and that is what he hopes to reach by this affirmation that "the dream is the realization of a desire."

This formula has several aspects, but all these aspects can be summed up in this way: it connects the dream to the concrete individual experience.

First of all, thanks to this formula, the dream is not connected to a general function, or rather, the allusion of this general function does not give an exhaustive explanation of the dream. To say that the dream comes from a diversion from reality, for example, is, for Freud, only a superficial explanation in the etymological sense of the word; one of the tainted explanations of this mistake of psychology which, as Freud likes to repeat, consists in not wanting to go beyond the manifest content of the dream; that is to say, beyond the conventional signification.[9] And, at the same time, even if it is true that Scherner goes beyond the manifest content, if only to see in the latent content the exercise of a general function, the disinterested game, so to speak, of a function like the imagination, it is also true that such a theory is not sufficient for Freud. What Freud says is that the dream is the realization of a desire. There again he could have fallen into abstraction. I can very well see a romantic theory of desire. We could personify desire and make it Desire, as Scherner personifies the fall of the concepts in the plastic representation, to make it the Imagination. We would then obtain a general and abstract theory of the dream-desire. We would move Scherner's imagination toward the desire and we would then say that the imagination transposes the thought into a scenario of desire, but in the scenario of any desire, as long as it is one, for, we would add as an axiom, the *Desire is seeking to be realized. . . .* We could then develop a symbolism of desire consistent with this general and abstract concept, a symbolism where the imagination would grasp the thoughts in the point of view of *possible* desire.

But Freud did not fall into this abstraction. The theory that I just imagined could not be Freud's, for in this theory the desire that will be realized would be, like the image of the dream with Scherner, the work of a free game of the Imagination at the service of Desire and, again, the desires such as they would be realized in the dream could not be connected to the concrete individual, being determined only by the fact that a general function is always stretched toward the realization of another general function.

That is why Freud's thought is different. It is not about saying that the dream is the realization of Desire in general, but the realization of a particular desire, determined in its form by the particular experience of a particular individual. If the child whom Freud talks about dreamed that he ate all the cherries, it is not because the Imagination, working on the mnemonic materials of the day before, found the "cherries" again and looked for, in the name of "Desire," the *possible* desire, but because this particular child had actually desired the cherries, which is very different.

And this reveals to us, at the same time, another aspect of Freud's formula.

If he had been satisfied by this amendment of Scherner's theory that we have imagined, Freud would still have remained in abstraction for a second reason. He would not have reached the concrete, because the desire would not have been an individual wish, actually coming from the individual; it would have been a *possible* desire, given the plastic materials of the imagination, and he would have missed this desire as being psychologically real, since it would not have been supported by the first person. But precisely, for Freud, the thought of the dream is a concrete desire, not only by its individual content, but also by the fact that it is a *psychologically real* desire, and from that, the *"I" remains constantly present in the dream.*

Scherner's theory goes beyond the overtly abstract theories of the dream and comes close to the concrete by giving a meaning to the dream, thereby seeing in it the revelation of something. But this revelation leads us only to the intimacy of a *psychological life in general*. If Freud had stopped at the idea of a determination of the content of desire by mnemonic materials, his theory would only have led us in the domain of virtualities of individual experience, and we would have been in the abstract, since we would not have gone beyond the level of possibilities. But Freud postulates an effective desire, determination by a real motive; he truly grasps then the psychological concrete, since he leads us to the very heart of individual experience.

But what does the term *desire* mean? Freud explains the mechanisms of desire (cf. 556 ff. and, in general, the whole section 3 of chapter 7) rather than answering this question, and he purposely withholds its specific development until the end of the work.

After explaining the technique he uses for the interpretation of dreams in chapter 2, he analyzes in the same chapter the "Dream of the injection given to Irma" (98–109). The manifest content is decomposed in its elements, and Freud notes the thoughts awakened respectively by each of them. As the story unfolds thoughts appear, shedding light on the signification of the elements of the manifest content, in such a way that if we confront these thoughts with the manifest content, the latter is to the former like a play to its theme, in this precise sense that the first ones express the idea of the wish and the second one the scene where the wish is accomplished. And, on the contrary, each time that, in the course of the *associations*, the idea of a painful situation appears, it is the opposite situation that is realized in the dream.

> I reproach Irma with not yet having accepted my solution; I tell her: if you are still in pain, it is your fault . . . The sentence I tell Irma gives me the impression that I definitely do not want to be responsible for the pain she is still feeling: if it is Irma's fault, it cannot be mine. Must we look in this direction for the inner finality of the dream? I am frightened by the idea that I could have neglected an organic disease. This fear is easy to understand for a specialist who deals uniquely with nervous people, and who is brought to blame hysteria for a host of symptoms that other physicians treat as organic diseases. Meanwhile, I do not know why, I have a doubt concerning the sincerity of my fear. If Irma's pains have an organic origin, their cure is no longer in my jurisdiction: my treatment applies only to

hysterical pains. Would I wish there to be a diagnostic error so as not to be responsible for the failure? (100 sq)

The analysis finished, Freud can present the story of the latent content.

> Here is the finished analysis of this dream.[10] During the work I resisted as best I could all the ideas with unconscious thoughts contained in it. I stressed an intention which the dream realizes and which was its motive. The dream realizes some desires which were awakened in me by the events of the evening (the news brought by Otto; the editing of the history of disease) [cf. preliminary story (97)]; the ending of the dream is that I am not responsible for the persistence of Irma's disease; the dream avenges me: it sends the reproach back. It takes from me the responsibility of Irma's disease which it refers to other causes [stated in details]. (110)

In a word, the manifest content, compared with the materials supplied by analysis, appears like a play that "ends well." "The dream," says Freud at the end of the part I just quoted, "exposes the facts such as I wish they had happened; its content is the realization of a desire, its motive a desire."

It is clear that the term *desire* is suggested to Freud by the fact that the latent content discovered by him represents an accomplishment and as, through analysis, we find, on the one hand, thoughts that pre-form this accomplishment, and on the other hand, feelings that call for it, either directly, or in pushing away the opposite accomplishment, Freud believes he can assert that desire is both the content and the motive of the dream.

As to the generalization of this affirmation, Freud realizes the difficulties it presents.

> If I assert that all dreams are realized desires and that there are no other dreams than those of desire, I know I will meet an irreducible opposition. It will be objected: the fact that there are dreams which we need to interpret as accomplished wishes is not new. . . . But to say that there are only dreams of desire is an unjustified generalization that we can refute easily. (124)

And not only does Freud come back repeatedly to this general objection, but it is precisely this objection that constitutes the dialectic ferment which, from chapter 4 on, allows him to develop his theory.

The most current objection to the theory of dreams as accomplishing desires consists in saying that "unpleasantness and pain

are more frequent in dreams than pleasure" (125). Outside of dreams
"which contain, during sleep, the painful emotional states of the
day before, there are still nightmares, anxiety dreams, where this
feeling, the most horrible of all, shakes us until we wake up. And
it is precisely with children, in whom we found the clearest dreams
of desire, that these nightmares are the most frequent" (125).

But Freud eliminates these objections by showing that they are
founded on the manifest content, whereas he is talking about the
latent content. "It is true that there are dreams of which the manifest
content is painful, but have we ever tried to analyze these dreams,
to uncover their latent content? If not, all the objections are un-
justified, for is it not possible that all the painful dreams and all
the nightmares are revealed, in fact, as dreams of desire" (125)?
And, in fact, it is to answer positively to all these questions that
Freud will introduce the notion of transposition and all the other
notions that constitute the components of his theory.

Freud's argument is first of all purely logical; he starts by alleging
the *possibility*, and it seems that the last word is left to induction.

"After the analysis taught us that behind the dream there hides
a meaning and a psychological value, we did not expect to see this
meaning interpreted in a unilateral way" (544). And it is thought
that we are going to limit ourselves to probabilities. In fact, this
is not the case. The movement of Freudian thought is bolder. The
idea that the dream could be a realization of a desire was revealed
to Freud following his analyses. It was from the very beginning
a marvelous working hypothesis, for it is because of this hypothesis
that we can approach the study of the dream according to the spirit
of concrete psychology. Freud has the intention of giving a solid
base to psychoanalysis by erecting in principle his working hypothesis. He does not feel secure in the shadow of induction; he needs
the certainty of the possibility of generalization, and it is in this
spirit that he approaches the question at the end of the work. It
no longer concerns giving "analytical" proofs, but about demonstrating that the dream *can only be* an accomplishment of desire
(cf. 560). Freud's last word in the discussion is that "the dream
is always the accomplishment of desire, because it comes from the
unconscious system that has no other aim but the accomplishment
of desire, and has no other strength but that of desire.[11] We finally
end up at the *unconscious*.

Even though this is the essence of Freud's thought on the possibility of generalizing his fundamental affirmation, we should not believe that he succeeded in completely erecting in theory the true motives of this generalization. We will see, in the chapter about Freud and the unconscious that theories of the kind I just mentioned cannot be connected to the true inspiration of psychoanalysis, and if Freud does it, it is because he expresses himself in a language that betrays his vision. Thus is that the quoted phrase is only a justificative dreaming in the style of a psychology of which Freud is the first to reject the consequences.

The true motives for this generalization, defended by Freud with so much tenacity in spite of all the objections, are found in the way in which the fundamental formula of the Freudian theory of dreams is modeled on the exigencies of concrete psychology.

Psychological fact, being a segment of the life of the particular individual, is inseparable from this individual. But it is *actually* inseparable; without which the continuity of the "I" is broken and there is no longer any psychological fact. Desire, however, does not connect the dream to the individual from the point of view of the content, but because it assures the dream precisely this continuity of the "I," without which psychological fact is just a mythological creation. If the dream is the accomplishment of a desire, it is only a variation of the "I" which dreams it and which, consequently, is constantly present. The desire assures the dream the continuity of this presence of the "I." In short, *through the theory of the dream-wish, the dream becomes an act.*

We see there again the incompatibility of concrete psychology with the notions of official psychology.

The psychological fact must be personal and actually personal, these are its conditions of existence. It follows that the fundamental notion of this psychology can only be the notion of the act. The act is the only notion — the only one of all notions — which is inseparable from the "I" in its totality; it is only conceived as the *actual incarnation* of the "I." And it is precisely for this that concrete psychology can only recognize the act as *real* psychological fact. The idea, the emotion, the will, etc., cannot be recognized by concrete psychology as having a psychological actuality, therefore as having concrete reality.

Freud holds to the theory of the dream-accomplishment, because this theory makes of the dream an act, an act of the particular subject whose dream it is, and because he does not see any other way for getting the same result, to assure the dream both the continuity and the actual presence of the "I." It is evident that Freud cannot express himself exactly in these terms. He belongs to another generation, his evidences are different from ours, he thinks about things differently, and he undergoes dialectical attractions that carry him away from the field of his true thought. But whatever the dialectics that he has to assume as his own, his discoveries are there and can indicate what, for reasons in no way lacking honor, escaped Freud himself.

VI

We understand, then, in the *Traumdeutung* the antagonism between two tendencies in psychology: the antagonism, on the one hand, of official psychology whose fundamental procedure is abstraction, and, on the other hand, of the Freudian tendency that is an orientation toward the concrete, but toward the concrete interpreted this time in a clear, sincere, and useful way for psychology.

It is this antagonism that explains the contrast between the knowledge of psychoanalysis and the ignorance of classical psychology.

If we start to separate the psychological facts from the singular individual, we place ourselves, right away, on an abstract level, on the level of generalities with which psychologists work. We will move among considerations that will stay beneath or above the particular individual, and as he alone can introduce into the theory the concrete diversity that makes it applicable to particular cases, the abstraction inevitably results in tautology, and it is chance that will have to fill the void created by the elimination of the individual concrete. Indeed, experience shows us only individual facts, but as we have condemned ourselves by abstraction to be able to get only generalities, we will be forced, in each individual case, to repeat generalities, and the explanation will be incapable of modeling itself on the fact to explain. Thus it is that, after having said that the dream is explained by the adventurous walk of an excitation on the cerebral cells, we can only repeat the same thing about each dream, and we have condemned ourselves not only to this tiring and ridiculous repetition, but also in not being capable of using the rich material that dreams supply us. In fact, the real use of this material can be found, for the first time, with Freud. In a general way, when we said that any psychological state expresses a state of the nervous system or is parallel to it, we closed the door to any concrete knowledge for opening the locks of the *Gehirnmythologie*.

If we start to take away the particularity of the fact, the conclusion will necessarily be abstract and will not be of any use in the comprehension of the concrete fact. Then the psychologist will not know anything. He will always have to repeat the same general conclusions about each particular fact: he will therefore never possess a real science; he will never be able to go beyond the level of language, and he will never do more than simply state that what happened in fact happened; tautology will always be the result of abstraction.

The psychoanalyst, on the contrary, since he never leaves the level of the particular individual, because for him the psychological fact is a segment of the life of the particular individual, will obtain concrete conclusions that will reach the facts in their particularity, and, consequently, the individuals in their concrete life. Not having made the mistake of abstraction, the psychoanalyst will acquire a true knowledge which, even if still imperfect, stands out because of its having gone through the concrete cases and particular situations.

The ignorance where actual psychology can now be found is therefore not a childhood disease, and no improvement is to be hoped from a *synthetic genius* or from the future in general. For this trait is not due to any imperfect methodology, which is theoretically efficient, but to the constitutive steps themselves.

Empirical knowledge, whatever it is, can only be established *a posteriori*, by extracting from the facts the teaching they contain. That is roughly the meaning of the term *induction*. Thus, to have productive induction, we must be able to use experience and not give it up from the very beginning. We need, in a general way, an empirical area adequate for the science in question. Without that, induction remains sterile, and will never result in explicative knowledge.

Classical psychology knows only sterile inductions. It tries to explain psychological life: for this, it would need to start from the very level of that life, that is, from the concrete individual and his acts, for this is the only way to acquire any knowledge that will be able to return to the individuals, and therefore to explicative knowledge. But instead, classical psychology begins by putting on blinders. It carves a formal and functional area into the psychological experience, and as this point of view represents only its most formal and most superficial aspect, the knowledge thus obtained is of no use for the comprehension of a concrete case.

Indeed, if induction is used in introspective psychology, it is uniquely to establish the manner in which, in the generality of cases, the *mental process* unfolds. We can take as an example the experimental introspection of the school of Wurzbourg. Here, we can, if necessary, talk about induction.[12] But what is it? It is about knowing what the characters of the image are, how it is thought of, what is its true role in the thought. The effort of the Wurzbourg school certainly represents progress. Classical theoreticians of the image like Taine, for example, always confused introspection and story-making. They invented the characters of the image to conform to the exigencies of the associationist and sensualist doctrine. The Wurzbourg school tried to find the answer by consulting the facts. It is progress. But the answer brought on by experience does not establish a *concrete* knowledge. We will end up knowing that the image remains vague, that Taine's images are excessively rare and may not even exist; that, in any case, the thought goes way beyond the image, and that it can even, in some cases, unfold without images. Experience answered[13] the question, but because the question was abstract, so is the answer. We had to gather information about the *form* of a psychological act and the answer to the question does not help psychology with making any real progress, for how does the fact of knowing that the thought does not resemble a film establish a "knowledge of the human being?" If there has been progress, it is simply because a group of sentences will no longer be spoken by psychologists. We have not acquired a knowledge that we will use for the comprehension of a concrete case. It is a knowledge with no possible application, because the only application that psychological knowledge is susceptible to is the application to the reality established by the concrete and singular individual. Thus, as it was not in the experiences of Wurzbourg, we cannot have it come out. For identical reasons, the results of abstract psychology still establish a knowledge without any possible application.

With Freud the induction is different. First of all, we start from the true psychological fact. Let us open any of Freud's writings: the report is always based on individual facts,[14] and what is essential is that the individual character, far from disappearing in the course of the explanation, always remains the main point. The psychology of the dream is based on the analysis of dreams considered as having individual meaning, considering the concrete individuals of whom they are the dreams. The theory of missed acts is based on the consideration of the missed acts as being the acts of a singular individual. The study of neuroses with Freud is not, as it is in classical psychiatry, a study of the *neuroses in themselves*, of these marvelous nosological entities that the individuals incarnate and for the study of which this incarnation has no importance, but on the contrary, each neurosis is like an individual act that we must explain as being individual. It is natural that in these conditions we end up with the constitution of a group of particular facts from which the generalization becomes possible, but one which, once made, becomes applicable to a multitude of particular cases, putting psychoanalysis in possession of a true knowledge.

We can quote as classic examples of Freudian inductions the manner in which the much-disparaged symbolism of dreams was established. It is the analysis of a large quantity of dreams that allowed Freud to establish this symbolism that does not have a universal value, but which, however, applies to the average individual, and even to everybody for some dreams. In this way, Freud has been able to interpret without analysis dreams that show up in everyone in a similar way and that Freud calls *typical dreams*.[15] Infantile sexuality, the Oedipus complex, the notion of transfer, of resistance, etc., were discovered in the same way. And it is because we start from the concrete individual that induction becomes possible; it is for the same reason that we can come back to the concrete individual, thus possessing an applicable psychological knowledge.

Such is then, on the one hand, the real antagonism between psychology and psychoanalysis, and such is, on the other hand, the real inspiration of the Freudian doctrine. We are now going to pursue our work in two directions. We will first state precisely the preceding affirmations by showing the components of the theory as they are given in the *Traumdeutung*.[16] But if these developments are going to confirm the idea that we had of the fundamental inspiration of psychoanalysis, they also will show that Freud did not always follow it faithfully. He falls back, indeed, with his notations and his theoretical speculations, into classical psychology.

Chapter Two

Classical Introspection and the Psychoanalytic Method

Chapter 2 of the *Traumdeutung* is devoted to the "Method of the Interpretation of Dreams." We know that this method consists essentially in this: 1) we separate the dream into parts; 2) the subject must tell, without critique and without reticence, everything that comes to his mind about each element of the dream. We might be surprised, as indeed we were, to see Freud apply such a method. Indeed, since Freud does not feel like studying dreams according to physiological methods, since he clearly asserts that he wants to use psychological methods, we would expect him to use introspection. But Freud does not use introspection but rather a method that we can only call introspective as a last resort and which, according to him, is just a variant of the method of deciphering (cf. 95).

The arbitrary trait of Freud's method has been objected to. The essence of this method consists in having the subject say everything that comes to him. On the other hand, the objection that psychoanalysts give currently to introspection is that even the most refined introspection cannot eliminate censorship, and since the aim consists in eliminating it, it is obvious that we need to replace introspection with another method where the thought is less falsified by censorship than in the waking state. The method will therefore essentially reside in the creation of a "psychic state which presents a certain analogy with the intermediary state between wakefulness and sleep and also, no doubt, with the hypnotic state . . ." (93), and all this because "from the moment we fall asleep, involuntary representations appear on the surface, because the action of the will and of the critique is relaxed" (94).

In fact, Freud moves away from introspection, because it could not be the method of a concrete psychology, and the opposition between introspection and the psychoanalytic method is again a particular case of the antagonism between abstract psychology and concrete psychology.

I

Let us omit all the classic arguments against introspection and let us assume that it is perfect: introspection can still only inform us about the *form* and *content* of the act that we introspect. I have forgotten a name that I am supposed to know well; if I introspect I will say that I feel a certain sensation of uneasiness, as I do a strong inner tension, the feeling of knowledge without verbal formulas and without image; some names come to my mind, but I push them away with a certitude full of resentment, the consciousness of this certitude, as well as the consciousness of my ignorance, make me feel perplexed until suddenly, without knowing why, I have a sensation of relaxation as if a resistance suddenly gave in and the word I was looking for appears at last, along with a feeling of relief. This is what introspection can teach me. But this is evidently sufficient only for abstract psychology. This psychology which is so careful to describe exactly the least nuances of all the feelings I had from the moment I realized the surprising omission until the moment the word appeared totally neglects the explanation of the fact in its particularity, and attributes, with no other concern, this fact to chance.

> If we were to ask a classic psychologist to explain why we often find it impossible to remember a name that we believe we know, I think he would just answer that proper names are more easily forgotten than other contents of memory. He would give more or less plausible reasons which, in his opinion, would explain this characteristic of proper names, not knowing that this process can apply to other conditions of a more general type. (*The Psychopathology of Everyday Life*, 3)

This means that the psychologist would attribute the omission to *general causes* which, whatever we do, can only be valid from a *generality*, but not from the *precise fact* that it concerns. And if Freud himself talks about "more general" conditions to which these processes can be applied, do not let this language be an illusion, for Freud only thinks of general factors, like censorship, repression, etc.; but the explanation he will give of each case will claim precisely to take up the fact to be explained in its particularity. Freud's fundamental postulate, from which all psychological facts are rigorously determined, has exactly the same signification.

It is natural that one who searches for explanations of this kind cannot be satisfied with introspection. Indeed, what did I do in my example of introspection? I considered the fact of forgetting from a *formal* point of view, so to speak, as if it had been about anything and by anyone. I did not take into consideration the fact that it was *precisely this word* that I had forgotten, and that it was *precisely me* who had forgotten it. My statements remain general and do not teach me anything, in that I do not know why I forgot precisely this word and at the precise time when I forgot it. But such is the nature of introspection. It cannot answer the questions of concrete psychology, because for that we need to consider the particular circumstances of the forgetting and what the forgotten word means to me; we need, in short, to consider this forgetting as a segment of my particular activity, as an act which, coming from me, characterizes me; we need, in a word, to get into the *meaning* of this forgetting.

But we will access the meaning of forgetting only if we possess the materials necessary to shed light on it. These materials, supposed to indicate the signification this forgetting has for me, can be supplied by me alone. But this cannot be done with the help of introspection, but exclusively with the help of a *story*.

Freud must then replace introspection by the story. The psychological fact being a segment of the life of a singular individual, it is not the matter and the form of a psychological act which are interesting but the meaning of this act, and it can be shown only by the materials that the subject himself supplies with a story.

We need to notice that the way Freud replaces introspection by the story is not simply the substitution of a concrete point of view for an abstract point of view, but also that of an objective point of view for a subjective point of view; to use this classical antithesis, and to speak a more modern language, with the use of the method of the story, Freud substitutes the point of view of *behavior* for one of *intuition*.

Indeed, if we replace introspection with the story, the psychological work will bear on "objective" themes. The story consists of objective material that we can study from the outside.[1] But we can say that this is only a trite objectivity. The true aspect of that objectivity is given only by the fact that the psychologist and his subject no longer have, as it is the case in introspection, the same function. The subject who submits to psychoanalysis ignores the interpretation, and he speaks first without doubting the meaning the psychoanalyst will reveal from the materials supplied to him. The introspective psychologist, on the contrary, expects from his subject a study that is already psychological, and he must always assume the presence of a psychologist in his subject. This is, we know, a striking difference from what happens in other sciences: for the mathematician does not expect a function to be a "mathematician," but to simply be a function, and the physician does not look for another physician in Ruhmkorff's coil, but only an induction coil.

The psychoanalyst does not ask his subject to change, so to speak, his way of being: he simply asks him to "let go" and to talk. The subject does not have to do anything else: the psychological work is for the psychologist, for whom, besides, the subject cannot do the work.

Finally, the method of the story is objective — and this aspect is even more important than the preceding one — because the psychologist is free from this "mimicry" that the rules of introspection impose on him. The "real psychologist" must, indeed, "sympathetically relive the states of the soul of his subject," without this, introspection does not make any sense, for it bears on facts which can only be grasped from the inside.

There is no trace left of that exigence except in the psychoanalytic method. For the latter wants to *interpret*, and determine the meaning of the dream, for example, with the help of materials supplied by the subject. And as the physician does not have to become a coil to study induction, so the psychoanalyst does not have to have "complexes" to find them in others, and he should not have any, for one becomes a psychoanalyst only after being submitted to a complete analysis. And what is remarkable, is that, because he only seeks interpretation, the psychoanalyst reaches objectivity, without having recourse to "spatial schemes!"

But the method of the story is not only opposed to the abstract and subjective character of introspection; it also represents the antithesis of its *realism*. Introspection, being capable of giving only the form and the content of a psychological act, has meaning only in the realistic hypothesis and, indeed, classical psychology considers introspection essentially as a form of perception. Its themes correspond to a *sui generis* reality, the spiritual reality or the inner life, and introspection must make us go through this "second" nature and inform us of its states. The themes of introspection, which are the ones of a reality, then suggest hypotheses on the structure of this reality and these hypotheses are also, naturally, realistic. We thus learn by introspection what is and what is happening in the spiritual world.

It is obvious that the psychological life of another individual is always presented to us only in the form of a *story* or a *vision*. The story, when it is expression through language (in all senses of the word); vision, when it is gestures or, in general, action. I am writing: there is a story here, as there is vision. I express, with the help of writing, "the states of my soul" of which a certain number can be guessed by the vision of what I am doing by the attitude I have while writing, the play of my physiognomy, etc.

The story and the vision have a practical and social function, and because of that, their *structure* is *finalist*: for me, language corresponds to a *significative intention*, and the actions to an *active intention*.

It is first under this *intentional* form that the story and the vision insert themselves in daily life. The story is taken for what it is; the significative intention for me corresponds, for others, to a *comprehensive intention*, and as to the vision, everyday life equally respects its level. I speak, and everyday life only sees the significative intention. I reach out for the pitcher of water, someone hands it to me. In the first case, I am understood; in the second one, a *social reaction* answers my *action*, and that is all.

In short, we do not leave, in daily relations, the *teleology of language*, and we stay on the plan of significations, comprehensions, and mutual actions.[2]

Classical psychology starts precisely by leaving this teleological plane and by omitting the significative intention. What interests classical psychology is not what the subject relates, but what happened in his mind while he was talking. It therefore needs a certain correspondence between the story and the *sui generis* processes. To find these processes, nothing is available but the story, but it surmounts the difficulty, by dividing it. We will have then, on one hand, the expression and, on the other, the expressed, but also two kinds of existence, because the expressed has a way of being *sui generis*: it is spiritual, it is thought.[3]

It is evident that this "thought" brings, in the point of view of the signification, nothing new: the signification of the idea and signification of the word is exactly the same thing. Only when we talk about the signification of the word, we did not yet leave the teleology of language, whereas the term idea precisely marks the transformation of the teleological point of view into a realistic point of view. Classical psychology divides the signification to go from the level of significations to the level of mental processes. It thus removes itself from the dialectics of everyday life and it makes of real entities what is only, in the point of view of this dialectic, a simple instrument.

One will object that the introduction of the idea brings something new, for the word is only an instrument of signification, and this signification in itself must be thought within an individual consciousness before it can be expressed. The idea, therefore, represents something new: a psychological act that must be described and studied. But this objection is nothing else but the description of the procedure that classical psychology accomplishes, the dividing of the signification once it is realized.

After the dividing, psychology omits the significative intention and places itself in the point of view of *functional formalism* to describe the mode of production of what is expressed, the way it is lived; the signification as signification is no longer important; it does not matter what is thought, for what interests the psychologist is *thought* in general.

II

According to us then, the classical psychologist proceeds in the following way: he divides the significative story and makes of its double an *inner* reality. Instead of keeping the ordinary attitude which is convenient to the teleology of social relations, he relinquishes it suddenly and searches in the story the image of "I don't know what" inner reality. Such is his attitude when he finds himself confronted with a story of another. But later he takes it back for his own story. All the changes will then be represented by the fact that it is not the *comprehensive* intention but the *significative* and *active* intention that he will have to renounce, and instead of doing the dividing for another, he will do it for himself. And once the dividing is completed, he will try to describe the inner reality from the point of view of functional formalism. He will then say that he *introspects*.

Introspection or reflection is nothing else but the abandonment of significative and active intention for the benefit of functional formalism, and this change of point of view corresponds to a second story, of which the starting point is established by the significative story, considered in the realistic and formal point of view. Objectively, introspection is nothing but a *second story* resulting from the application of the point of view of functional formalism to the *significative story*; and what psychology seeks is precisely the substitution from the first story, purely significative, for a second story which has no longer anything to do with the teleology of human relations, which is, from this point of view, purely "disinterested" and must constitute the description of a *sui generis* reality.

We need, in short, to choose between two hypotheses. We can say first of all that what is primitive is introspection, for it is my psychic states that I first know and I can only assume psychic states in my peers because of my own inner experience. If that is true, it is artificial to say that I divide the story, for all I do is endow my peers with these states which, for me, really constitute the *double* of the story. The fundamental step of introspective psychology would not therefore be the *dividing of the story*, but an *analogical reasoning*.

The second hypothesis consists of admitting that what is primitive, is, on the contrary, the realization of the story by means of dividing and not of introspection; far from representing a spontaneous attitude, the latter would only be the application to oneself of an attitude taken toward the significative story by "common sense." And in this case it is not analogical reasoning, but the division which characterizes psychology. Only, this division can go either toward others, or toward oneself, and it is this second case that we call *introspection*.

We know that psychology owns the first hypothesis. It is still this hypothesis which inspires the attacks directed against it: it is precisely analogical reasoning for which behaviorists reproach classical psychology.

But several considerations direct us toward the second hypothesis. First of all, we need to distinguish introspection as it is in *principle* from introspection as it is in fact, for we must not confuse the introspective method as it is practiced now and as it was practiced in the past with the professions of faith concerning introspection. Thus, it is introspection as it is and as it has been that we are looking at and not the different *promises* of introspection.

And besides, we need to distinguish the simple *inner perceptions* such as organic pain and organic needs as they happen in the continuity of daily life, of *systematic introspection*, as it is used in psychology. This distinction is necessary first, because "suffering" stems from "life," while introspection stems from knowledge,[4] but especially because introspection, as a psychological method, goes beyond the frameworks of the simple ordinary perception of our inner states. For the very fact of talking about the "perception of my inner states" already implies abstraction. What is immediate, is the suffering, but such as it happens in the sequence of the events of my daily life.

If we consider the question so defined, we might notice that introspection does not proceed from the inside in a way that is as spontaneous and as sincere as psychologists usually state. For it is obvious that the psychologists of the preceding generation, when they supply us with the syllogism in the chapter entitled "Psychology of Reasoning," reveal nothing that is really *internal*, since it is logic, Aristotle's logic, whose method is not at all introspective, which taught us the existence of the syllogism. It is evident, then, that if the psychologists in question believe that they have dealt with the psychology of reasoning, it is uniquely because they divided the story. And since it is absurd to assert that the syllogism is an "immediate theme of consciousness," it is evident that, at least in this case, introspection came, so to speak, from the outside, and that the second story was constituted by the pure and simple dividing of the first one.

We know that the psychologists in question always confused introspection and confabulation, that they copied their psychological realities from language: doesn't the demonstration of all these points form an integral part of Bergson's doctrine?

Only we think, and Bergson is the first, that there is a mistake in the *way* in which we used introspection, but that true introspection is something else.

This is only a hypothesis in which we are carried away by the naive character of psychological realism.[5] The least we can say is that nothing condemns the idea which states that what we call mistakes committed in the usage of introspection is only the revelation of its true essence, which appears even better to the degree that the ones who use it are more simplistic. This would not be the first time that the true character of a scientific procedure appeared with clarity precisely in a theory that has already been condemned.

Bergson also showed that the introspection of his predecessors was not sincere, that their introspective stories fed from the fulfillment of theoretical exigencies. Only, he only saw one avoidable mistake, and, considering the character of his undertaking, he could not see anything else. But the Bergsonian critique could very well mean that the *exogenous* character of introspection has already been demonstrated for a certain kind of *second story* that makes *static* persons intervene in his scenario. Bergson only institutes a new kind of second story, a new technique of elaborating impersonal dramas: he works with *dynamic* and *qualitative* persons, and the themes that his formalism develops and the language in which his realism is expressed are different; but there really is *ignoratio elenchi* in assuming that this kind of second story escapes the critique that ruined the first one, for the Bergsonian introspection has never been submitted to an examination similar to the one to which he submitted the introspection of his predecessors.

But what comprises the likelihood of the classical opinion the most is the primacy of the *teleological attitude*. For it is the comprehension and the interpretation which come first, and psychology only comes later. The expression and the comprehension imply neither an inner *sui generis* experience on the part of the one who expresses himself, nor the projection of the themes of this experience in the consciousness of the one who is understood. Such an interpretation of the expression and of the comprehension implies not only the realism but also all the procedures of classical psychology.

It is onto the teleological attitude that realism is grafted. And still it is practiced first in general: introspection comes in third place, representing the application to itself of realism which, in theory, is practiced first in regard to others. And let us remember, too, that historically the notion of introspection appears relatively late. Then our hypothesis might not appear so absurd — or at least we will notice that the problem here is not the one of psychology by introspection, but psychology of introspection.

Be that as it may, these developments go beyond the limits of the present study.[6] What matters to us here is the content of introspection and the comparison of the content of the *second story* of classical psychology with the one that psychoanalysis supplies. But, regardless of the last word about the true mechanism of introspection, it remains true that it is indissolubly tied to abstraction and to formalism. And that is sufficient to discredit it in view of a psychology that wants to be concrete and productive.

III

What characterizes the method used by psychoanalysts, on the other hand, is that it does not comprise the realistic procedure that we tried to describe. The psychoanalyst does not leave the teleological plan of significations, therefore he does not invent a new and paradoxical attitude, such as reflection. His aim is different: he wants to prolong the attitude of everyday life until it reaches concrete psychology; he does not try to transform the plan of signification into *realities* but to expand it to rediscover, at the base of *conventional collective significations*, the *individual significations* that no longer go through the ordinary teleology of social relations, but reveal individual psychology. The psychoanalyst will then also have a *second story* to contrast with the purely significative story. Only his second story will not result from the disarticulation of the first one but will only represent its expansion. We will only consider then, in theory, the significative intention, but a significative intention which does not take us into the area of social interactions but into the psychology of the concrete individual. The second story of classical psychology takes us toward *realizations* whereas the second story of psychoanalysis moves simply toward *interpretation.*

"The scientific theories of dreams do not take part of the problem of interpretation, since, for them, the dream is not a psychic act, but an organic phenomenon revealed only by some psychic signs" (88). For abstract scientific theory for which representations have their own existence, the problem of interpretation cannot be posed. Interpreting, then, means nothing else but connecting the psychological fact to the concrete life of the individual. For Freud, on the contrary, the problem of interpretation cannot be posed, since he returns to a concrete conception of psychology.

All the dream is for "scientific" theory, which considers the dream abstractly; the entire dream is contained in the verbal formulas which constitute the story of the dream. Consequently, only by a story consistent with the formal point of view, will this theory be able to complete the story made by the subject. It will not need to bring in the hypothesis of a manifest content and a latent content. Freud, on the contrary, considers the dream as a "psychological fact, in the real sense of the word," as a segment of the concrete individual life; he therefore must admit that the verbal formulas do not express in the story what they would express if they were detached from the subject, but precisely something of the subject. He will have to go beyond the conventional signification of the formulas which the dream uses to rediscover the concrete individual life, and will therefore have to oppose a story created in terms of individual experience, to the story in conventional terms, a deep story to the superficial story; he will need to bring in the distinction of what the dream *seems* to express and of what it *really* means.

Freud calls the conventional story manifest content, and the translation of this story in terms of individual experience, latent content (cf. chapter 2, 79–104 *passim*).

If we want to understand psychoanalysis in all its particularity, it is necessary to expand this distinction. It is not enough to say that its concrete character essentially consists of the adoption of the point of view of the signification, because this point of view in itself is rich in applications which can go, as with Spranger, in a very different direction from the one we want to point out here.[7]

Freud likes to repeat that the way in which classical psychology habitually characterizes the dream as incoherent, fanciful, illogical, in a word, devoid of meaning, comes from the fact that we were accustomed to considering only the manifest content of the dream. And, indeed, after having given the dream some unflattering names, classical psychology goes immediately to the formal and functional statements. It does this in accordance with the abstract steps we have tried to describe. In dream theory, however, the classical theories do not totally omit signification, because it is, on the contrary, the realization of the impossibility of giving a meaning to a construction that is as crazy as the dream that determined the model for theories like those of Binz and Dugas.

Behind this attitude, there is an implicit postulate, in that the terms of the story that the subject makes of his dream have their ordinary content; that when, for example, the key word appears, its signification coincides with the ones indicated in dictionaries.

In a general way, psychological facts, even though they are actually "psychological," still only have their conventional signification, their signification so to say "public." I am talking to a woman, and suddenly I wipe my mouth: this gesture has no other signification but that of "general-gesture-of-wiping-my-mouth," and all that the psychological explanation can make is a statement consistent with the point of view of functional formalism. It is this same postulate that is at the base of all the judgments on the psychological facts that seem to have missed their conventional signification. The dream is incommensurable with the categories of conventional significations, thus it has no meaning. I have forgotten a proper name that I know very well: classical psychology sees there only a missed recall, thus something purely negative.

We are confronted with a true general postulate of classical psychology, the *postulate of the conventionality of signification*. It is the intervention of this postulate that Freud wants to indicate by saying that classical psychology wants to consider only the manifest content.

This postulate is intimately tied to realism and to abstraction. It points the way to realism and opens the door to abstraction and to formalism. To abstraction, because it is conventional significances which are realized, given that realism proceeds by divisions and that what is divided is the conventional signification. I say "because."

There is in this a *feeling of relation* for psychologists. In addition, once the conventional signification is realized, abstraction and functional formalism enter. Abstraction, because realization in a particular individual's consciousness does not change anything in this signification, and the fact of finding itself in *this* consciousness precisely *now* has no importance for classical psychology; whether it is about me or someone else, psychology will devote itself to identical statements.

These statements are made in the spirit of functional formalism. They concern connecting the realized signification to its *class*: we will connect "because" to the class of the *feelings of relation*, and we will later describe the general circumstances of the production and the way in which this feeling of relation is "lived." We know that some psychologists have displayed much subtlety in this kind of exercise.

We understand, therefore, that classical psychology falls back on quality, and that it can seek the individuality of psychological facts only in the qualitative irreducibility of the act in which they are lived. Everything happens as if every individual consciousness had exactly the same content of significations, as if each individual consciousness was only the intuition of significations, always the same ones and for everybody significations that the intuition would grasp without changing anything. It is evident that there is, in these conditions, only *manifest content*; that is, conventional significations, and all the effective work remains reserved to functional formalism: how would we explain, if this were not so, the fact that psychologists are not interested in the "meaning" and that they fall back uniquely on the abstract and formal study of the realized signification? For the point of view of meaning has too many consequences, and it would purely and simply have brought psychology to psychoanalytic discoveries. In any case, it is not through any particular grace that Freud discovered psychoanalysis: it was "simply" a matter of realizing that the classical method of psychology broke apart on some special cases which imposed a concrete point of view, and that this point of view would have led anyone to the same discoveries. Let us not say then that classical psychology, too, has known of the point of view in question. Our preceding affirmations are justified. It is much too easy to show, once a discovery is made, that it did not fall from the sky like a meteor, but that it was announced. Then why have we waited for the discovery to notice the "annunciation?"

It is true, however, that once the realization was accomplished, the point of view of meaning intervenes in classical psychology. But it intervenes only when it is ordered by abstraction and the postulate of conventional signification.

It is ordered by abstraction when it concerns preparing materials for the psychological study. Once the realization is accomplished, we proceed to a first transformation: depending on their significations, we bring the terms of the story back to notions of class. I just exclaimed: "Darn, still another match that won't light!" "Darn," means *emotional state*; "still," *feeling of relation*; "match," *image*; "won't light," *perception*. The whole thing is a *judgment*. We will then try to find out if there has been analysis or synthesis — synthesis preceded by an analysis or analysis of the primitive synthesis of the perception — but in any case, the signification will already have disappeared. I know that "modern" psychology is no longer present; I know that I cut things in pieces, and that I have given too much importance to the solid elements; but whether we say that we have here a simple placing of a verbal formula of a unique and indivisible attitude, or anything else of this kind, the fact remains that the attention leaves meaning and moves toward the formal study of functions or attitudes: *only the language is different*; the procedure is the same.

Classical psychology also has individual significations. But they are only related in the way in which the psychological fact is lived by the individual, in its qualitative *unicity*. But this *ineffability*, which should represent the *summum* of the concrete, comes from functional formalism and in fact contains no determination that is properly individual; the concrete it represents is only general.

But the true role that "meaning" plays in classical psychology appears only if we push the analysis of the postulate of the conventional signification further. We have just showed how this postulate is linked to the fundamental steps of classical psychology. But we can wonder about the origin of this postulate.

Realism consists of the division of conventional signification; that is, in its projection to the inside. The problem of the meaning is thus eliminated once and for all, because it is precisely to conventional signification that psychological reality belongs, since it is the one projected on the screen of inner life. But, on the other hand, why is it precisely conventional signification that is realized?

What is primitive in theory is, as we have said, the teleology of human relations. But *common sense* adopts vis-a-vis this teleology the same naive realism as it does with regard to the *themes of perception*. The difference comes only from the fact that perception is divided toward the outside, while conventional signification is divided toward the inside, but there is *hypostasis* in both cases, and the naive realism of metaphysics corresponds to the naive realism of psychology.

It is evident that the essence of this realism is constituted by *social anthropomorphism*. For it is the collective value of language and of acts that is realized as spiritual fact. And this realism is naive precisely because the transition from the point of view of social finality to actual reality is achieved without any justification, and with a certain spontaneity. There is, in fact, almost no "transition": it is the "jealousy of Society" that this realism expresses; the individual is only the accomplishment of social exigencies; in other terms, the category of "Reality" is very naturally open first of all only to the social aspects of things.

Classical psychology, by the use of the postulate of conventional significance, only prolongs the attitude of this naive realism. This attitude might have suited science. But this is not the case, and all sciences have gotten rid of it. Only psychology has kept it. It sets itself free with great difficulty from social exigencies, and the postulate in question is not the only example of the transformation of these exigencies into realities. If Freud had a hard time having infantile sexuality recognized, it is precisely because physicians and psychologists wanted to see in the child only what he *should* be according to certain well-known collective representations.

In any case, the conservation of an attitude condemned by all scientists shows that the mind of psychologists is not yet sufficiently "fashioned" for truly scientific work. Malebranche said, "Our reason may be Christian, but our heart is pagan." It is the same with psychologists: they speak of science, they copy it, but *they do not like it.*

IV

The postulate of the conventionality of signification does not have any relation with experience. The different dialectics that a word can carry are given by language, on one hand, and, on the other, by the state of the sciences — they can be categorized at all times. It is evident that to establish this cataloguing, no properly psychological study is necessary, since everything is given by objective documents in the simplest sense of the word. With the postulate of the conventionality of signification, psychology assumes that these dialectics are the only ones which exist, and we can establish the list without any consultation of the really subjective themes. It is then with good reason that we talk about "postulate," since the belief in question could not have been suggested by experience, as the question could not even be asked because of abstraction. Consequently, the idea that there could be a purely individual dialectic from which individual acts borrow a purely individual signification is totally foreign to classical psychology; it does not conceive, for example, that the word engaged in the network of significations of an individual context can acquire an original significative function, in the same way as it acquires a conventional signification when taken in a network of conventional significations.

Conventional significations are not, of course, all situated on the same plan. On the contrary, they consist of superimposed layers which go from absolutely conventional significations toward significations which are less and less so and assume an individual experience more and more closely. We could even establish for each term what we could call the *pyramid of meanings*, an upside-down pyramid, of which the base would be represented by the meaning that the term has for everyone and the top by the one that it can only have according to the experience of only one individual. Between the top and the base are located the meaning which, while not being determined by the experience of just one individual, do not belong to everyone. "Hat," for example, means "head cover" for everybody, "gift" only for some people, and "sexual parts of the husband" exclusively for the woman whose dream Freud analyzed in the *Traumdeutung*.

We are forced to interpret into practical life; otherwise the mutual adaptation that human relations suppose is impossible. All significations except for the properly individual signification are given by collective experience. We learn that the hat is a head cover and that we can give it to someone as a gift: these are inductions which supply us with the materials of our daily interpretations. But these interpretations go beyond the conventional significations only in exceptional cases, for they rest on spontaneous inductions which reveal only what can happen again in an obvious way in social life. Scientific psychology itself does not go further. It stops at the spontaneous inductions which give us conventional significations and seeks nothing else: that is why it is so shallow. Psychoanalysis, on the contrary, is not satisfied with that; it is precisely the individual signification that its interpretation seeks. Its method may seem whimsical and arbitrary, for all it does, in reality, is to prolong these interpretations that we practice every day; but instead of his locking himself in the limits outlined by the teleology of human relations and the spontaneous inductions that can supply materials only to find the *conventional* signification, the psychoanalyst organizes an inquiry to obtain the materials necessary for the constitution of the *individual* signification. The psychoanalytic method is nothing but a technique allowing one to expand the significations consistently with the exigencies of concrete psychology. It is from this point of view that the different procedures that constitute it need to be explained.

V

Since it is the individual signification of the terms of the story that interests us, we need to approach the dream as a text to decipher. Indeed, to the extent it is signification, the structure of the intimate signification is exactly the same as that of the conventional signification, and when we want to find the former we do not need to proceed in any other way than when we try to establish a given signification. We therefore need elements and guide marks; in short, a context. Besides, if there are intimate significations, it is because the individual possesses, so to speak, a *secret experience*. We need, then, to probe this secret experience, and we will obviously probe it only to the extent that the subject will supply us with the materials that it is made of. Thus arises the necessity of the fundamental step of Freud's method: *free associations.*

This term *association* can create a misunderstanding, or, rather, an illusion. The illusion exists with Freud, and this fact has been exploited by those who, into the "modern mobilism," jump at the mere sight of the word "association." In fact, there is a lot of meanness in this dragging on about the superiority of the *fluid* over the *solid*, and it would be truly prudent to devote ourselves to more important problems, especially since there are here only two versions of the same mythology.

There is, in *free associations*, neither associations, nor freedom.

Psychology has got used to talking about association where there is no consciously admitted significative intention and where the subject is not inspired by any dialectics. I am writing; I am conscious of a significative intention, and I am in some way supported by a dialectic: my ideas on the question that I am dealing with. But let us suppose that I suddenly stop and I renounce both my significative intention and my dialectics. My consciousness will not empty itself because of that; other ideas will follow, and I may even have a lot of ideas, but I have nothing more to "say," and my ideas are no longer organized by one of these laws which usually give our thoughts their "structure"; that is, I no longer have any significative intention, and the continuation of my thought is no longer consistent with any of the "classical" dialectics, that is, conventional ones. We will then say that I have *associations*, and we imagine that the ideas follow each other consistently with certain affinities, being purely mechanical. It is therefore very clear that, in this example, we will speak of association only because we did not recognize any of the classic dialectics, and therefore we speak by virtue of the postulate of the conventionality of the signification. The idea that, if we ignored conventional dialectics, what we are in the habit of considering as a rational continuation would in the same way seem to us to be "brain dust" (as, for example, when ignorant people qualify as "gibberish" the writings of difficult philosophers) and that, consequently, if we speak of association and brain dust, it may be because we do not know this dialectic that acts when we have renounced all intentional dialectics, and is foreign to classical psychology.

It results from the *experiences of association* that the *associative series* never goes adrift, but that the subject always revolves around certain intimate themes.

"... It is completely inaccurate to pretend," says Freud (523, cf. 521, sec. 3, to 524, sec. 2),

> that we let our representations go adrift when, at the time of the work of interpretation, we meditate and allow the involuntary images to appear within us. We can show that we only renounce the representations of the objective that we know and that, those being stopped, others, unknown, or, according to the less precise expression, unconscious, manifest their force and determine the course of the involuntary images. Our personal influence on our psychic life does not allow us to imagine a thought devoid of objective; I do not know the state of psychic disturbance that could allow it.

It is therefore evident that Freud will opt for the hypothesis contrary to that of classical psychology: he assumes that as we have renounced all significative intentions and all conventional dialectics, our thought will continue to be ruled by a dialectic and to translate a significative intention; but this dialectic and this intention are original; they are no longer conventional, but intimate. The thought then keeps on having signification even though, conventionally, it does not want any. It therefore has a structure, although it seems to have renounced all structure, and, in that way, it is as rich in teachings as when it functions consistently with conventional dialectics.

There is therefore no need to talk of association, and it is not even logical to talk about it. And yet Freud does it as well as traditional psychologists. As for psychologists, we now know the procedure which produces their illusion. We take the terms of the story and we project its contents in the "inner life" to realize it and to have its idea. We then reverse the order of events, and we think that the facts followed an opposite past to that of analysis: speech expresses the idea, and if the words were connected, it is because the ideas that they bear were first *associated*. And as for Freud, he talks of association first in virtue of this procedure, and, also, because, consistent with the exigencies of classical psychology, he would like to translate, in associationist language the assumption, or rather the fundamental fact on which his method leans, as it is clearly shown in the text that we just quoted.

But by accomplishing the associationist step, Freud abandons the inspiration of his own method. He is only interested in the significations of verbal formulas which constitute the story. He therefore should not leave the teleological plan to fall into realism; he should limit himself to the ordinary interpretation of language, but not to go beyond the meaning to penetrate inner life.

When the psychoanalyst asks the subject to tell him everything that goes through his mind, without critique and without reticence, he asks nothing else but to abandon all the conventional editing, to strip all technique and all art, to let himself be inspired by his secret dialectics.

As for the dream, it represents a creation of this personal dialectic; that is why it was a mystery for classical psychology, which wanted to approach it with the postulate of the conventionality of the signification. And, since it is so, the analysis of the dream can only use states with a similar origin; that is, where we rediscover the personal dialectic. And the story starting from the events of the dream must show us how these are inserted in the secret experience of the individual.

An essential teaching emerges from this comparison of introspection with the psychoanalytical method.

There are two ways of using the *story* of the subject. We can disarticulate it by abstraction and formalism to project it in one way or another into the inner life. This is the attitude of classical psychology.

Or we can use the psychological themes simply as the context of a meaning for which we search: we recognize here the attitude of psychoanalysis.

This results in a very important consequence for the attitude of the psychoanalyst himself: the hypotheses of structure are forbidden to him. He has no right, seeing the true character of his attitude, to look for mechanisms, for whatever is at this moment the paradox of this affirmation, it is toward a psychology without inner life that psychoanalysis leads us. However, as we have seen concerning the representation that Freud makes of the mechanism of the story, we will see later that he did not notice this consequence of his attitude.

CHAPTER THREE

The Theoretical Frame
of Psychoanalysis and the Survival
# of Abstraction

By examining in the first chapters of the Traumdeutung the way psychoanalysis approaches the facts and the spirit in which it conceives its study, we discovered a radical antagonism between Freud's attitude and that of classical psychologists which opposes one against the other two irreducible forms of psychology, concrete psychology and abstract psychology. For the very way in which the problem of dreams is presented implies a definition of the psychological fact that moves the interest of the spiritual entities to the dramatic life of the individual, and the method as it is conceived by Freud turns away from the investigation of the inner reality to deal only with the analysis of the "drama."

Because of this concrete attitude, Freud is led to make a certain number of discoveries all the more amazing in that they remained inaccessible to classical psychology: these discoveries demand an explanation.

We would expect, then, to find in Freud explanations adapted to this concrete psychology he founded; to find in the explanations, the concrete attitude that presided over the discoveries. This expectation is all the more legitimate in that we cannot see how the notions of abstract psychology could suit facts the mere discovery of which already assumes the negation of the spirit in which these notions were elaborated.

Psychoanalytic speculations do not live up to his expectation. Everything happens as if Freud, by his explanations, wanted to go backwards through the path that the concrete inspiration of psychoanalysis made him travel, and he wants, in some way, to be forgiven for his concrete discoveries by giving an explanation in the taste of classical psychology. The fundamental antagonism between the two forms of psychology can be found in the heart of psychoanalysis itself, which thus appears as if torn between the old psychology and the new psychology.

We easily conceive that it is essential, by seeking the psychological teaching that psychoanalysis contains, to insist on that point. It is not enough to notice the presence in psychoanalysis of a concrete inspiration; we also need to show how far it goes, and how and why its influence stops when we approach the explanations. That is necessary not only to show that the true critique of psychoanalysis consists in judging it in the name of this concrete psychology that it institutes and not through such and such a trend currently fashionable in official psychology, but also because this sharp conflict between the concrete attitude and the abstract attitude within psychoanalysis will allow us to define and push further the affirmations of the preceding chapters.

I

The dream is the accomplishment of a desire. The formula is still general and Freud does not stop at this statement. He will not make us believe that it concerns just any desire; he will, instead, try to show that the majority of the desires that are accomplished in the dream have something in common: they are infantile desires. "... We are surprised to find *in the dream, the child who survives with his impulses*" (176).

But this time it seems that if Freud does not leave the term desire undetermined, if he gives it the determination that we just saw, it seems, I say, that the *dialectical ferment* no longer exists simply in the exigencies of concrete psychology, since its first formula is satisfying in this regard, but in *inductive* necessities. The desire that the story allows one to reconstitute is tied to an infantile memory or to an infantile impulse: this seems to result purely and simply from analysis. It is no longer a question of principle, but a question of fact.

That is why, when Freud tells us: "We are surprised to find," there is no reason to think that this is not just talk, but we must believe, on the contrary, that he is perfectly sincere.

Concretely, the question is presented in the following manner: the distinction between the manifest content and the latent content will allow Freud to examine the particularities of the memory of the dream, particularities "often noticed, never explained" (151). These particularities are: 1) the preference given by the dream to recent time and to indifferent time; 2) the frequent intervention in the dream of infantile memories that we do not have during the preceding day (cf. 151–52).

The intervention of the recent time — that is, the presence in the dream of events of the day before that are indifferent in appearance — is a fact to be explained, and not, as many believe, the very explanation of the dream. Indeed, to explain the dream by the force of the persistence of the recent memories does not give us the reason of the precise scenario that is realized in the dream and does not teach us anything about the individual life of the subject whose dream we want to explain. Freud will explain the particularity in question by *displacement*.

The manifest content represents only the latent content, and

> the psychological process because of which an insignificant incident is able to be substituted for important facts can seem singular and questionable. We will explain, in a later chapter, the particularities of this operation, which is incorrect in appearance. It is sufficient here to examine the results; countless experiences of analyses of dreams have compelled us to admit them. It seems, seeing this process, that everything happens as if there were a displacement, let's say, of the psychic accent . . . The psychic charge goes from representations of which the initial potential is high to others whose tension is weak; these can thus cross the threshold of consciousness. (163)

But displacement is just an instrument in the transposition of the dream. "The fact that our dream, so stirred up by important events, is woven of indifferent impressions of the day is explained here again by transposition" (161). It is the same for the mechanism of condensation that Freud defines a little further (165).

But as we said earlier, we are now in the area of induction. We have become acquainted with the general model of the theory; it is now time to qualify it and articulate it with regard to empirical necessities. The remark that we made about chapter 5 will also apply to all chapters, up to the "Psychology of the Processes of the Dream." Our task from now on, is to explain all the facts consistently with the conceptions that the first four chapters tell us about, by properly modeling the ideas upon the facts.

If the way Freud will articulate his thought is dictated by *inductive* necessities, the latter can still only give the reason, *but do not explain the precise form of the notions that Freud brings in*; these notions are explained, on the contrary, by the conception that Freud has of the relations between the manifest content and the latent content, and the form of psychological existence that suits the latter: these are ideas that will constitute, from now on, the keystone of the *Traumdeutung*. If the first four chapters cannot be understood without the recognition of the exigencies of concrete psychology, the rest of the *Traumdeutung* can only be understood through the ideas that Freud has on the latent content and the way we must interpret its existence. We must therefore insist on this last point. We will see then that Freud could not escape the constitutive steps of classical psychology. As these steps are in obvious opposition to the concrete inspiration of psychoanalysis, this opposition allows us to recognize them and to look at them. Psychoanalysis will then provide us with an education which, though negative, is nonetheless precious: we will learn to recognize the abstract essence of certain notions that appear at first as being derived essentially from the experience itself. Freud points out that it is not necessary for the analysis to be integrally a reconstitution.

"What we need to retain," he says (526),

> from the objections made, is that it is not necessary to attribute all the ideas which arise in the course of the work of interpretation to nocturnal elaboration. At this time, we retrace the path which leads us from the elements of the dream to the thoughts of the dream. The work of the dream has done it in the reverse sense and it is unlikely that the path can be followed both ways. It seems rather that, during the day, we practice by our new associations some sort of soundings which sometimes here, sometimes there, touch the intermediary thoughts and the thoughts of the dream.

Something of the associative material has effectively been thought, but what? and in what way? This is the problem.

Freud answers that the act which consists in thinking the latent content is a psychological act, but this psychological act is without consciousness.[1] The distinction between the latent content and the manifest content leads us to the hypothesis of the unconscious.

Here is the approximate scheme of the Freudian answer. The *free associations* or the *story* give remarkable material in two ways. This material is first disproportionate relative to the manifest content; it is also revealing, for it allows the subject to learn about things that he himself ignores and which meanwhile belong to his intimate life. As it is the subject who gives the latent content, rich in details and unexpected in its signification, we must, so to speak, give it back. Freud reverses then the temporal order: of the story resulting from the analysis, he creates the thought of the dream and later conceives it as previous to the manifest content, to the dream itself. And precisely because the thoughts of the dream do not belong to the available thoughts of the subject, they do not have an existence similar to the manner of being of the *available* thoughts but a different manner: the form of their existence is unconscious. This is how the fundamental theoretical notion of psychoanalysis, the notion of the unconscious, appears in the *Traumdeutung*.

"What is stifled persists and subsists in the normal man and remains capable of psychic output," and "the dream is a manifestation of it, theoretically it always is, and it practically is in most cases." In a general way, "*flectere si nequeo superos, acheronta movebo.*" Interpretation is the royal road that leads to knowledge of the unconscious in psychic life (596).

It is this realistic conception which is at the base of all of Freud's speculations. It necessitates first the introduction of the notion of transposition. If the latent content represents a psychological reality previous to the manifest content, previous in right and in fact, only a labor of transposition can explain the gap which exists between the two contents. But once we have recognized the transposition to explain the gap, we must expand the question and explain the precise nature of this gap. There is a first fact; that is, that the gap bears first on the psychic value of the elements. An element whose conventional signification is very small can in the dream represent a psychological signification of great intensity. It is a fact, and we saw that Freud introduced the notion of *displacement*. In addition, the gap is quantitative as well as it is qualitative: the associative material is very considerable, whereas the story of the manifest content is very short. That means that the dream "condenses." But the dream condenses in yet another sense: "There is in the elaboration of the dream a sort of constraint which unites the patterns in one whole. . . . It [this constraint] presents itself as a part of another primary process: condensation" (165). In a general way, we will just have to erect in theory the different aspects of this gap to end up with new notions, and that is what Freud does.

But the distinction between the manifest content and the latent content and the manner in which Freud conceives it still necessitate speculations in another direction — the cause of the transposition. We have to know the cause of the "disguising in the dream":

> why wouldn't indifferent dreams, which from analysis were revealed as being dreams of desires, express these desires clearly? The dream of the injection given to Irma, that we talked about at length, didn't have anything painful, it appeared to us from analysis as the very clear realization of a desire. But why was an analysis necessary, why doesn't the dream find its meaning right away? In fact, the dream of the injection given to Irma did not at first give the impression of fulfilling a wish of the dreamer. The reader will have noticed it, I did not even know it myself before analyzing it. If we name this fact as the transposition in the dream, a second question will be asked right away: where does this transposition come from? (126)

Truthfully, the very position of this question does not necessarily lead us toward concrete psychology, since, as Freud remarks, an abstract answer is equally possible: "We could," he says, "at first sight, imagine diverse answers. This one, for example: it would be impossible, during sleep, to find the expression which would correspond to the ideas of the dream" (126). What would explain the scenario of the dream would be this powerlessness; the dream would then be a sort of stammering. Against this theory, Freud calls on experience: "But," he goes on, "the analysis of some dreams makes us give another explanation for this transposition." The "uncle's dream" will show that the transposition seeks to hide painful thoughts.

If Freud is fighting the theory that he points out, it is not exclusively for "experimental" reasons. The very fact that, without stopping at the indicated theory, he asks another explanation from the facts, shows very well that he feels the abstraction of the theory in question. If we adopted this theory, the dream would again become something general, and the explanation will not be able to reach the particular dream in question, and the particular individual whose dream it is. On the contrary, the way in which Freud will answer the question will at least permit the exigencies of concrete psychology to draw near, if not to satisfy them.

The theory that Freud rejects is *sterile*: it immediately halts research. Once we have said that the dream is a stammering, we could only repeat this general affirmation about each dream and about each element of the dream, and be amazed, at best, by the varieties and the whims of this stammering. The way in which Freud answers the question necessitates new ways of interpretation and will have him expand on hypotheses concerning the structure of "the psychic device." That is why he can say: "We have here the feeling that the interpretation of dreams could give us, on the structure of the mind, some notions that until now we expected in vain from philosophy" (134).

Freud will then undertake notional works that will be pursued parallel to the *inductive* ways that we have pointed out, to be resumed later in a systematic way in the "Psychology of the Dream Processes."

II

But once the answer to the problem of transposition has been stated, we will notice in Freud a certain return to abstract psychology.

"The transposition is intentional, it is a process of dissimulation" (131). A group of thoughts need to be expressed in the dream, but instead of appearing such as they are, they are hidden. We notice at the same time that the thought of the dream is painful to the subject, that he has a tendency to hide from the responsibility which falls to him from the very fact of having dreamed. It is this last observation which will allow Freud to explain the transposition.

Since the latent content is real, and besides, since what is conscious is only the latent content in disguise, it is necessary to admit that the form of existence of the latent content is *unconscious*, and that consciousness is obvious to the representations only under certain conditions. For clarification, Freud introduces a metaphor taken from political life: a censorship watches over the entrance of consciousness. Freud understands very well the dialectics of his stance: as the latent content is psychologically real without being conscious, not only will we no longer be able to define the psychological facts by consciousness, but also, because of censorship, consciousness will grasp the psychological fact only in a distorted way and the assimilation of consciousness to a sense organ will become *possible* with all the consequences of such an assimilation. "The fact of becoming conscious," says Freud, "is for me a particular psychic act, distinct and independent of the appearance of a thought and of a representation. Consciousness appears to me as a sense organ which perceives the content of another domain" (133). Freud asserts further, very clearly, the relativity of perception through consciousness. "The unconscious is the psyche itself and its essential reality. Its nature is as unknown to us as is the reality of the outside world, and consciousness informs us of it in a way that is as incomplete as our sense organs on the outside world." (600) Consciousness has a specific energy. This specific energy is nothing but censorship.

When we talk about the relativity of sensory knowledge, we want to stress two things: first, the fact that, considering the number and the choice of sense organs, our knowledge of the outside world is essentially selective and even incomplete; then, by the "specific energy" of the nerves, sensation makes the givens of experience sustain a qualitative deformation.[2]

It is very important to point out that, from its starting point, the affirmation of the relativity of perception through consciousness has, with Freud, a very particular orientation. There are philosophers who assert the relativity of the inner experience; Kant's ideas on this question are well known. But, with Kant, we are concerned with the theory of knowledge. The cause of relativity with Freud, however, has first of all something moral and even sociological. If we take Freud's thought on the question from its starting point, we find that *consciousness means responsibility*. The subject feels responsible for the content of his consciousness: any conscious psychological fact is an act for which the subject must accept the responsibility. It is what explains censorship and repression, and this is the cause of the relativity of consciousness.

There are, indeed, thoughts which are painful for the subject: he represses them; that is, he does not want to be conscious of them. Thus, it is not the act of thinking which is painful; a repressed thought is not painful in the simple doing of the act which consists in producing it, for a repressed thought can always be thought in itself, as long as the subject does not have to bring it back to himself; it becomes painful only if the subject has to bring it back to himself, if it appears as the expression of a way of being which implies for him indignity and decay, because, for example, it is contrary to the "idea of *me*."

Indisputably, we find here the seed of a concrete conception of repression and of all the attitudes it implies, or, at the least, we remain at a level where repression can have a *concrete* meaning. By expressing ourselves as we just did, our affirmations, whatever their vagueness, are relative to the acts of a particular subject, and we are in the presence of not mere representations but the very forms of which the subject would like to become a part; in the presence of a conflict not between mere representations but between ways of being, some of which are real but condemned, and others desired but unrealizable. *Consciousness*, such as we now consider it, is something other than a form of experience; it is essentially an act of recognition, of responsibility, even of identification — in short, this aspect of individual actions by which their connection to the "I" becomes evident and their recognition effective.

If Freud had directed his developments in that direction, he would have noticed that this *dynamics* of the representations that censorship, repression, and resistance assume relates to the very knowledge that the subject can have of his own behavior, and so the limitation of consciousness would have meant only the negation of the omniscience of the subject vis-a-vis himself, negation that the psychoanalytic method already implies.[3] Under these conditions, Freud would not have needed to conceive, on the one hand, a world of unconscious psychic entities and, on the other hand, to make consciousness an organ of perception.

Freud does not stop at these concrete possibilities, and he immediately applies to consciousness the classic scheme of the relativity of perception. And we will see that when he studies the problem systematically, we will only find the abstract unfolding of this model.[4]

We need to add that Freud speaks in terms of *representations*, of *effective states*, etc., and this language then takes him completely into the field of influence of classic psychology.

This is particularly obvious in the "Psychology of the Dream Processes" (Standard Edition). The analysis of this chapter where we will see Freud as torn between abstract psychology and concrete psychology will be very instructional.

III

It is with section 2 (527–43) that we need to start. Section 1, where Freud studies the omission of dreams (509–27), has great technical interest, but we would only repeat what we have already said about the concrete character of the inspiration of psychoanalysis, and denounce, as we have done above, its illusion concerning the mechanism of the story. With section 2, we get into the very heart of Freudian speculation. It is only here that the problem is stated with all necessary clarity.

> Let us put together the main results obtained until now. The dream is a complete psychic act; its province is a desire to fulfill; the failure of recognizing this fact, the peculiarities of the dream and its multiple absurdities come from the censorship it underwent at the time of its formation — the obligation to condense the psychic material, the necessity of representing it by sensorial images, and, though irregular, the preoccupation of giving to this whole thing a rational and intelligible aspect. Each of these principles leads to postulates and to conjectures of psychological character; we need to examine which are the relations of the desire and of the four conditions of the dream, as well as the relations that these have with each other; we need to insert the dream in the sequence of psychic life.

Here is the problem and the plan of the chapter.

Freud starts by the analysis of this particularity of the dream which consists in dramatizing the thought. "In the dream a 'thought,' most often a desire, is objective, staged, lived. . . . How may we explain this particularity of the expansion of the dream, or at least how may we get it into the sequence of psychic processes" (528).

Before even answering the question, and more to the point, to answer it, Freud expresses the fact in the language of classical psychology. "If we press the analysis closer, we will recognize in the manifestations of the dream two characters almost independent from each other. One is the figuration as being actual and leaving no room for doubt; the other the transformation of the thought in visual images and in speech" (528). The second character, which appears only in dreams, means for Freud that ". . . the representative content is not thought about, but is transformed into perceptible images" (529). Thus, to explain the dramatization in the dream will consist in describing the mechanism of this transformation. We can easily foresee the general terms of this explanation. It is evident that, seeing the way in which Freud formulates the fact, the scheme of the sensualist tradition is used. It is this classical scheme of psychological work, going from sensation to thought, which is present in Freud's mind. There is, besides, the realistic conception of the latent content which shows us the work of the dream going from the thought of the dream to the images of the manifest content. It is then natural that the dream appears to Freud as a regression. There remains only the elaboration of the conception of the psychic device so as to make *progression* and *regression* possible. For that, Freud needs a topical representation, liable to have, later, reservations placed on the degree of reality which suits such a representation.

"The great G.-Th. Fechner, in his *Psychophysics*, expresses, after some considerations, the hypothesis that the scene where the dream happens may be other than the one of the representations of the day before. . . . The idea thus offered is that of a psychic place" (530).

"Let us represent then the psychic device as an instrument of which we will name the components: instances, or, for more clarity, systems. Let's imagine then . . . that a constant succession is established, by the fact that the systems are traveled through by the excitation in a certain temporal order . . ." (530). As we foresee it, the model of the reflex will intervene to state the thought precisely. Freud says it very clearly:

> All our psychic activity starts from excitations (outer ones or inner ones) and ends up at innervations. The device will then have a sensitive extremity and a motive extremity. . . . The psychic process usually goes from the perceptive extremity to the motive extremity. . . . But this is only the realization of an exigence known for a long time, according to which the psychic device would be built as the reflex device would be. The reflex would be the model of all psychic production. (531)

The results of the analyses now makes Freud introduce new differentiations in the psychic device. "In what we have said until now about the composition of the psychic device in its sensorial extremity, we did not have intervene either the dream, or the psychological explanations that can be deducted from it. But for the knowledge of another part of the device, the dream becomes a source of argument" (533). That other part is the motive extremity. It is the notion of censorship which will force Freud to introduce a new differentiation: the preconscious. Indeed, "as we have seen it, the instance which criticizes is in closer relation than the instance criticized with consciousness. It rises like a screen between it and consciousness." And Freud will now situate, for classical reasons, the conscious and the preconscious at the motive extremity.

> We have found some guidemarks that let us identify the instance which criticizes with the guiding principle of our waking life, the very one which decides our voluntary and conscious actions. If we replace these instances by systems which accord with our hypotheses, the system in charge of critique finds itself being brought into line with what we have seen at the motive extremity . . . We will call preconscious the first of the systems at the motive extremity, to indicate that from there, the phenomena of excitation can reach consciousness. . . . (534)

"This is at the same time the system containing the keys of the voluntary motility. . . . We will give the name of unconscious to the system placed farther back; it could not access consciousness unless, it goes through the preconscious and, during this transition, the excitation should yield to certain modifications" (534 ff.).

Freud's thought is clear. He introduces in the psychic device the notion of the unconscious to situate the thought and the inspiration of the dream, and the notion of the preconscious to make it the place of the activity of censorship — transposition and elaboration of the dream. We have not yet reached the explanation of regression, and yet the abstract character of the Freudian hypotheses is already obvious not only in the fundamental scheme, but also in the way in which it is mentioned by Freud.

If Freud places censorship near consciousness, it is first because, as we have indicated above, consciousness means above all responsibility. Without this, we do not understand the necessity of admitting at the beginning of [perceptual] consciousness a censorship which is not a simple condition stemming from the theory of knowledge, but essentially a selection made, not with laws which state the behavior of an automatic process, but in accordance with *principles* that examine the forms from the point of view of their signification. If Freud places consciousness itself at the *motive extremity*, it is not exclusively in virtue of the scheme that he uses, but essentially because motive extremity means action, and it is consciousness that takes the responsibility for it. In this way, the Freudian structure means deep down, that action is possible for the subject only in a *presentable* form. In the preconscious, the responsibility finds itself grappling with forms; that is, with the sense of budding actions. The term *action* is meant, of course, in the largest sense of the word; it then means a "fact" of the subject, whichever it is. In considering things from this point of view, we are, in some way, on the level of concrete psychology.

In reality, Freud expresses himself in a language that makes the concrete disappear. First, hardly has he declared, for the motives we have just indicated, the formula *motive extremity*, than right away and definitely it will mean to him only *motility*; it is no longer a question of the individual, human action; the word act has lost its dramatic and human sense, and even all sense in general: it is for Freud only what it is for the physiologist, a movement, or rather movement in general, a new form of excitation. We are now on the plan of *functional formalism*: the term *excitation* will often come back in its physiological signification, and without any trace of humanity. Freud, forgetting more and more that his theory is true only to the extent to which it participates in the concrete, to the extent to which it recognizes as a psychological fact only what is an effective act of the singular individual, will strive more and more to explain things by a mechanism which should be psychological, but which, in fact, as do all psychological mechanisms, functions in empty space.

"We will call *preconscious* the last of the systems at the motive extremity, to indicate that from there the phenomena of excitation can reach consciousness with no delay, if some other conditions are fulfilled, for example, a certain degree of intensity, a certain distribution of the function that we call attention" (534). And at this moment he will also make away with the concrete character of his theory of the relativity of consciousness to give it a purely mechanistic version.

"We will give the name of *unconscious* to the system placed farther back, it could not access consciousness, *unless it goes through the preconscious*, and during this transition the excitation should yield to certain modifications" (535).

It is in this language that Freud formulates the problem for one last time before resolving it:

> We cannot describe the step of the hallucinatory dream other than by saying: the excitation follows a backward path. Instead of being transmitted toward the motive extremity of the device, it is transmitted toward its sensorial extremity and it finally gets to the system of perceptions. (535)

But how to explain this fact? In truth, Freud does not explain it. "We just gave," he says, "a name to an inexplicable phenomenon." What he gives us are glimpses, very interesting ones, concerning the orientation of his thought.

First, Freud would willingly see the explanation of the "hallucinatory character" in a purely mechanical fact, in appearance at least, that is in the *displacement of psychic intensities*. His idea then verges on the thesis according to which all the difference between the current reality, on the one hand, and memory, on the other hand, shows as a difference of intensity — the analysis shows us that the psychic intensities are "displaced." It would be enough then for the psychic intensity to be displaced from a representation to a sensorial image for the latter to become hallucinatory. "When," says Freud,

> we talked about the work of condensation in the dream, we could not hide from the hypothesis that during the elaboration, the intensities inherent in the representations are entirely transferred from one to the other. It is probably this habitual modification of the psychic process which allows one to occupy the system to be occupied by perception until there is the full sensorial vividness, by following a reverse step, beginning from the thoughts.

There is not, properly speaking, a pure and simple identification between actuality and intensity. The Freudian theory, not having at its origin the classical problem of the difference between the sensation and the image, does not as a rule imply this thesis, condemned even by abstract psychologists, according to which the image is only a weak perception and the perception a strong image. Freud borrows the model of his theory from this vulgar statement, that thoughts, to hold our attention, must be of a certain "interest," that they must possess, to use his favorite expression, a certain energy of occupation. We will then talk about the psychic level that the excitations should reach or about a threshold that their intensity, also "psychic," must go beyond, but it remains understood that this psychic intensity is not to be confused with the physiological intensity.

Only Freud, by placing himself squarely in the formal point of view, finally ends up at the thesis in question.

Consistent with abstraction, he starts first by abandoning the meaning to keep only the representation. From that moment on, the intensity itself becomes something formal: it becomes a "quantity" tied to a representation and, being something other than the bare representation, it becomes *mobile*. It is precisely this mobility that explains the *displacement*: the psychic intensity can pass from one representation to another to give it an "energy of occupation" capable of going "to the full sensorial vividness."

Whatever the problem about knowing whether or not Freud fell back into the thesis in question, it remains — and that is more important — that Freud, too, substitutes an impersonal drama for the concrete drama, and that in the theory of displacement, it no longer concerns the concrete individual, but only autonomous evolutions, so to speak, of this property that psychology recognizes in the representations, namely the intensity.

Freud ends up by giving the term *regression* its complete sense, but complete in the sensualist point of view. The dream backtracks the path of the knowledge which goes from the sensations to the thoughts. "The assembling of the thoughts of the dream finds itself disintegrated during regression and brought back to its first matter."

The identification of regression with the reverse process from the one which, according to sensualists, lets the thoughts emerge from the sensations, thus closes the circle of abstraction: in this thesis, there is no more trace of the concrete definition of the psychological fact and of the necessity of connecting the dream to the life of the individual in particular. A simple disintegration of the thought is only, indeed, a blind process, purely mechanical, where we no longer see the participation of the "I"; in short, the process in question can no longer be an act of the particular individual. The associationist dialectics led Freud much too far: *at the base of the dream there generally appears a process.*

Freud likes to repeat, as do physicians, that his theories simply represent convenient matters of speech, and that he is ready to abandon them for a more convenient representation. He could, certainly, say the same thing about the preceding theories. But, the theories in question are *convenient* only if we work with the evidence of classical psychology, and in any case no expression that is oriented toward deadend streets can be convenient. And this is the case of the expressions in question. For being abstract, they only invite us to build *psychic* mechanisms which, though realistic, are nonetheless unreal. Indeed, no psychological reality can be recognized to the "displacement of psychic intensities" or to the "disintegration of thought," for the processes in question are in the third person: the explanation goes "from thing to thing," it implies the action of the representation, even the action of its intensity, which implies in turn the position of the representation or of its intensity *for itself*, and, as only the action of the subject can be *real*, the theories in question are psychologically impossible. Freud therefore commits the classic mistake: he breaks down the act of the subject into elements that are all under the level of the "I" and then wants to reconstitute the personal with the impersonal — or, if we prefer, he makes hypotheses of structure when hypotheses of structure are forbidden to him, and he builds them in accordance with the realistic model, that is, in projecting into the *inner reality*, under its general form, only what is needed to clarify the act of the subject.

Freud could very well say that these developments in question do not make of the dream "something in general," for they only express the "implications" of the dream, and do it without any prejudice about the concrete attitude of the interpretation itself. That is perfectly true. In fact, the possibility of the interpretation does not at all imply an analysis of regression. We can interpret the dream without making any hypothesis about regression: the dream is an act of the subject and we must simply know what it means. However, the position alone of the problem of regression already implies abstraction, since the problem can only be asked if we examine the dream through the notions of class of classical psychology, consequently if we place ourselves in the point of view of functional formalism: it is only then that the illusion of the reality in the dream appears as a "regression of the representation to the sensorial images." Freud's thought is triggered not by necessities inherent in his doctrine, but by purely temporal contingencies. He must fight the theory that makes of the dream an anomaly by showing at its base, regular processes that make of it "a psychological fact in the real sense of the word," but unfortunately he thinks he must show that these processes are explained by "the ordinary laws of psychology," that is, by impersonal dramas.

An abyss is thus created between the practical attitude and the theoretical attitude of the psychoanalyst. The psychoanalyst founds, indeed, true steps on false principles by translating his fruitful discoveries into perfectly sterile models. This explains why the distance between the facts and the explanations is so great, and that it can be filled only by great ingenuity. We thus introduce into the heart of psychoanalysis an inner contradiction that bursts apart at each moment.

IV

These remarks can be very well illustrated by the analysis of complementary explanations that Freud gives of regression.

There is no regression during the day. Then "what change will render the regression impossible during the day? Here we will just settle for hypotheses" (537). But these hypotheses are perfectly abstract. "It is probably about changes in the distribution of the energy inside the different systems which then become more or less usable for the step of the excitation." It is enigmatic, but we will not see anything else clearer until the end of the paragraph. Freud senses this and points it out:

> This first part of our psychological utilization of the dream does not perhaps seem entirely satisfying. Let us console ourselves by thinking that we have to lay the foundations of our edifice in the dark. If we do not get completely lost, we will be able, starting from a new point of view, to end with similar results which, this time, will appear with more clarity. (543)

Meanwhile, psychoanalysis shows through even in this paragraph, only to get spoiled in abstraction.

Scherner had also noticed "in the dreams a vividness or a particular wealth of visual elements" (540). But to explain it, "he admits of a state of inner excitation of the visual device." Freud cannot go as far, at least not without explanations. For whatever his final respect for abstraction, he asks of it to be modeled after the results of his analyses. The end result is that regression is not just "any" simple disintegration, as we would believe it from Freud's preceding formulas, but that it has a determined orientation; that it is not a simple "degradation of thought," due to the dissolution of its superior forms, but that this degradation itself is, so to speak, informed by a "sense" that has a determined direction. Indeed,

> we can distinguish three kinds of regression: a) a topographical regression in the sense of the system exposed here; b) a temporal regression, when it concerns recapturing old psychic formations; c) a formal regression, when the primitive modes of expression and of figuration replace the habitual modes. (542)

"But then, if we remember the role which goes back to the events of childhood or to the dreamings founded on these events in the dream; if we remember how many times the fragments of these facts show again in the content of the dream, how many times the wishes of the dreams themselves are derived from them . . ." (540); and, above all, if we remember that in the dream it is the child who survives with his impulses (176), then "the dream appears as a return to the farthest past of the dreamer, as a revivifying of his childhood, of tendencies and instincts which have dominated it, of ways of expression that it disposed of" (542). There we feel a sort of relief: the term regression is taken in a living sense; what is stated here goes over the framework of the little hallucinatory game. Here, it is no longer a question of the transition from the idea to the image, and from the memory to the hallucinatory perception, but of the rebirth of a previous form of the individual's life, with everything that a way of being and living in a certain way implies, going beyond ideas, images and perception. It is no longer a matter of fragmenting the attitude of the elements that are under the level of the "I," and consequently impersonal, but of the return of the whole "I" to an older form, or rather its recapturing of this form. We do not throw away the form to give the elements an independent life of which they are incapable, but the form remains in the foreground, and the elements only play their role of element in the staging of the attitude, and their role of "scouts" in the analysis.

Unfortunately, abstraction again takes the upper hand, and the fact that regression is above all the rebirth of the child will be simply used to talk about the mechanistic theory. And as he is again seeking a hypothesis of structure, Freud will insist on the fact that the visual memories try to be reborn and practice a sort of selective attraction on the thought of the dream. But the memories of childhood are living impressions, and because they are living, they still keep a sensorial vividness. "It is a known fact that with people who otherwise have no visual memories, the first childhood impressions preserve, until an advanced age, the character of sensorial vividness" (539).

The memories of childhood that interest the psychoanalyst are the repressed ones. But the entrance of consciousness is equally forbidden to the thoughts that are tied to it. Then "this memory carries with it, so to speak, the thought to which it is tied and which has been hindered in its expression by censorship, into the past where it can be found" (539).

In this way, regression is, "everywhere where it is manifested, an effect of the resistance which prevents thought from having access to consciousness by the usual path, at the same time as from the attraction that memories exert on it which have kept a great sensorial vividness." Regression is then only a simple *deviation*. It is no longer about saying that the subject has, so to speak, relived certain events in terms of an old form. It is not the subject who acts, it is the representation that has dug itself a new path toward consciousness. It is not surprising then that, after showing Scherner's theory, Freud adds: "we should not be against this hypothesis; we will be satisfied in acknowledging such a state of excitation[5] uniquely for the psychic system of visual perception; but we will show that this state of excitation is a product of memory, the reappearance of a visual excitation which was actual in its time" (540).

Finally, all hope to witness the reappearance of the deep sense of regression disappears; it is the mechanism that will explain everything. "These three kinds of regression really only make one come together in most cases, for what is older in time, is also primitive in the formal point of view and is situated in the psychic topic, the closest of the extremity of perception" (542). This leads Freud to unfortunate ideas on the phylogenetic past.

Since, as he has just said, "what is older in time is also primitive in the formal point of view," Freud cannot help himself from showing us the *hallucinatory regression* at the origin of psychological life.

"The psychic device could reach its actual perfection only after a long development. Let us try to bring it back to a previous state" (551). The first structure of this device is of a reflex device,

> it could then immediately sharpen all sensation on the motive path. But life disturbs this simple function; it gives the impulse which leads to a more complex structure. The great needs of the body appear. The excitation provoked by the inner need looks for an outlet in motility. The child who is hungry will either cry desperately or will be restless. But the situation will remain the same . . . There can be change only when, one way or another . . . we acquire a calming experience which terminates inner excitation. An essential element of this experience is the appearance of a certain perception (food in the chosen example) of which the image will remain associated in the memory of the remembrance of the excitation of the need. As soon as the need is represented, there will be, thanks to the established relationship, the start of a psychic movement which will once again occupy the image of this perception in the memory and will again provoke the perception itself; that is, will reconstitute the situation of the first calming. It is this movement which we call desire; the reappearance of the perception is the satisfaction of the desire. . . . (537)

But the shortest path toward the accomplishment of the desire is precisely this mechanical hallucinatory evocation, at the time of the pairing of the desire, of the image of the satisfying perception. "Nothing prevents us from admitting a primitive state of the psychic device where this path is really covered and where the desire, consequently, terminates as a hallucination" (537). And we see how "the adaptation to life" will necessitate transformations by revealing the transitory character of the hallucinatory satisfaction. We will need, from then on, to close the road on the hallucination and obtain, to make the excitation deviate, "a better use of the psychic forces," that is, the maintenance of the exterior of the satisfying excitation. But, then, "all this complicated activity which goes from the memory image to the reestablishment of the identity of perception by the objects of the outside world is just a detour made necessary by the experience of fulfilling a desire."

The biological orientation of the Freudian scheme appears very clearly: at the beginning was the desire born from organic need. A classical principle, which we call principle of economy, or principle of pleasure, immediately intervenes: the desire seeks its immediate realization by the hallucination. And thus it is that in the beginning were the desire and the hallucination. "Nocturnal life has gathered what used to be in the past our waking life, our young and unskilled psychic life, a little like our children perpetuate the arms, today outdated, of primitive humanity, the bow and arrows. *The dream is a fragment of the childhood of psychic life, today outdated*" (538). Though these last formulas are similar to the one where, earlier, we had to recognize the inspiration of concrete psychology, we should not have to believe that they mean the same thing, for all the preceding developments are destined simply to give them an abstract signification. The revivifying of childhood meant earlier the revivifying of certain determinated attitudes that characterize childhood — the revivifying of an attitude "with human form" that the individual *effectively* had in his childhood and which reappears in his dreams with a staging borrowed from his present life. But now that Freud has showed us the beginnings of "the psychic device," the same formula means the rebirth of a *mechanism* that no longer has a "human form," the rebirth of a "process" that no longer interests the subject, but only the step of the representations and of the excitations.

We hardly need add that from the point of view of concrete psychology Freud's glimpses (since he does not want us to take them as an explanation) are again unintelligible, at least if we take them literally and if we put into effect, even slightly, the mechanisms that he introduces.

First of all, what can this attraction of childhood memories mean? It is always convenient to say: hypotheses are only matters of speech, or *hypotheses non fingo* and, while supporting this point of view against the critique, acting and writing as if we took his hypotheses seriously. All this only represents oratorical precautions. If there was no intention of having these hypotheses taken seriously, none would be made.

As we cannot give the psychological facts an efficiency other than that derived from the subject, they must be capable of appearing as forms of the action of the subject. But we will look in vain for an individual act that can correspond to this attraction Freud talks about; it is impossible to formulate it in the first person. As with the description of the mechanism of regression, it does not, at any time, leave room for the intervention of the "I"; the mechanism therefore functions in empty space.

In addition, a whole series of formations admitted by Freud in his explanations concerning the expansion of the dream presents the disavantage of being psychologically empty. These are the constellations that are preliminary to the formation of the dream (cf. especially 582–84).

Since Freud starts from a realistic conception of the latent content, it is natural to see him assert that the most complicated activities of thought can occur without the knowledge of consciousness (582) and that, from the fact that our judgment rejected some thoughts because they seemed wrong or useless for an aim temporarily pursued, a process can result, ignored by consciousness and which will go on until sleep. . . . Let us say that we call this process *preconscious* (583). We have then in the preconscious "a sphere of thought left to itself," (584), since not only is it not occupied by consciousness, but it is also abandoned by the preconscious occupation. It is true that unconscious desires can take over these thoughts, but the question is knowing how they can be psychologically real, when this occupation by the unconscious desires has not yet occurred. Freud simply answers that consciousness and psychological fact are not synonymous, and he adds, also, that the old postulate of the unity of the soul or of consciousness is refuted by the facts. But the question is not there. Are these thoughts, abandoned to themselves, still the acts of the "I?" But that is impossible. The continuity of the "I" is particularly broken here, for these preliminary constellations are only floating thoughts and we only have to observe Freud's language to see that they have some autonomy. But in this case, they cannot be *psychologically* real.

V

The history of the successive differentiation of the psychic device and the postulate according to which "at the beginning was desire" suggest the same remarks. If efficiency does not extend integrally to notions in the third person, it is true nevertheless, that we are in an abstract area. The process that finally explains the dream is no longer susceptible to being individually qualified, so that Freud deserves here a reproach, exactly the same as the one he is used to giving to others. The term of the explanation is represented by general notions such as the biological needs of the organism, the adaptation to life. In a word, the theory does not come from psychoanalytic inspiration, since, instead of having us advance in the knowledge of the concrete individual, it goes back to, for example, biology. Also, we are more and more involved in an area where representations, excitations, energies, evolve with a sort of sovereignty, as if the whole was not meant to be an individual action. In a word, we penetrate farther and farther into inner life, biology, even physiology, but in a psychologically blind area.

It is then that we find these unfortunate formulas that are explained only by weakness with regard to the need for an explanation, and by the fact that, where the explanation is not indicated by the facts, we call forth notions in which, as in a heroic myth, we invest all of our enthusiasm. "Our biggest theoretical interest," says Freud,

> goes to the dreams capable of waking us up. . . . We wonder how the dream, in conscious desire, can disturb sleep, the accomplishment of the preconscious desire. *There has to be there relations of energy which escape us. If we knew them, we would no doubt see that to leave the dream alone and to give it only a detached attention, requires less energy than curbing the unconscious, as during the day before.* (567)[6]

"This awareness depends on the orientation of a certain psychic function, the attention which, it seems, can only be dispensed in small quantities."

We believe that a certain quantity of excitation, which we call energy of occupation, starts from a representation of an objective and follows the associative paths that it has chosen. This occupation has never been granted to abandoned, neglected thoughts; it was taken from stifled, rejected thoughts; all of them are abandoned to their own excitations. (538)

Indeed, all these formulas mean something, since Freud acts consistently with the statements that analysis supplied him. We could even translate a large part of these affirmations into a more concrete language. However, evolving among these notions, we are far from the "meaning" and from the psychological fact, "segment of the concrete individual life."

VI

The Freudian explanation of repression will show us the way Freud expands his theoretical constructions.

As with regression, repression is a primitive process of the psychic apparatus, and is explained, in the last analysis, by the great principle of the search for pleasure and of the escape from the unpleasant. Repression is not intentional at first and has nothing to do with responsibility: it is the functioning of a simple biological mechanism.

> The processes of the system, including those of the preconscious, lack psychic qualities; that is why they can appear as an object to consciousness only to the extent to which they lend themselves to its perception of the pleasant and of the unpleasant. We will have to admit that these releases of pleasantness and unpleasantness automatically govern the step of the processes of occupation. (565)

"We wrote," adds Freud further, "that only desire could make our apparatus move and that the course of the excitation was automatically governed by the perception of pleasantness and unpleasantness" (588).

During the time that we are considering, however, hallucinatory regression is the natural, immediate path. But as regression is sterile, a *second system* must intervene to transform the sterile hallucinatory energy into useful energy, that is, producing calmness. We can, if we want, make a comparison here with Bergson. There is in the human being a tendency to damage himself in the dream; the necessity of adaptation to life tears him away from it. This is a common idea to both Bergson and Freud, but also to a whole era. Freud, however, makes of the necessity in question a "system of the psychic apparatus," to be able to use it later in the explanation of repression.

This stopping by the preconscious of the excitations, which came from the unconscious, in view of the adaptation, is not the image of real repression.

In the simple escape from memory, the cause of repression resides in the unpleasant to which the experience gives a memory. And then, there is no more desire. That is why the escape from memory is not true repression. True repression occurs when there exists an *emotional transformation*, for, although the satisfaction of a desire initially provokes pleasure, satisfaction can only be unpleasant for

some others. Only, the cause of this repression is not simply what
is unpleasant such as it is, but one of a higher level. It depends,
indeed, on a judgment of the preconscious (592 ff.).

> In what way and under the influence of what impulse can this
> transformation occur? We just have to point out the problem of
> repression. Let us maintain that this emotional transformation occurs
> in the course of development (let us think about the appearance of
> dislike which, primitively, does not exist with the child) and that
> it is tied to the activity of the secondary system. (593)

This explanation shows us that Freud turned, this time again, toward
schemes in the third person. And it is obvious that the ideal explanation
which he wants to arrive at would consist in explaining everything
in an energistic way, by displacements of intensities, transformations
of energies, elevations and falls, charges and discharges of occupation, by the different adjustments of the different currents of
excitation.

After all, Freud succeeded, with much ingenuity, it is true, in
going backward in the path he followed in the preceding chapters
of the *Traumdeutung*. It is not simply a metaphor. In accordance
with the traditions to which he is tied, the dream of synthesis is
clearly present with Freud. He refers to it from time to time, by
saying that the analysis of the dream should be accompanied by
its synthesis. That would be, indeed, the great verification. We also
feel, in the chapter on the "Psychology of the Dream Processes,"
that he goes to hypotheses only in the hope of rediscovering, by
starting from them, the facts from which he began. Unfortunately,
he only touches *deductive* psychology. If he had seriously attempted
the *descending dialectics*, he would have seen that we could never
draw from these hypotheses the facts on which they are based, for
the mechanisms that he describes have the defects of the mechanisms
of classical psychology: they are not capable of determining the
individual, but only the general.

Be that as it may, once "The Psychology of the Dream Processes"
was completed, everything was assimilated in the *psychic*; everything
became a game of excitation and of representation: Freud succeeded
in building an edifice in the taste of classical psychology. He does
not agree with all the points of this psychology. For having made
some discoveries, he felt forced to enlarge the classic frameworks.

It is in this way that he felt he had to assume a group of processes at the base of the dream that it is not possible to attribute to consciousness. So, by attributing them to other instances, the psychological formations are finished before consciousness intervened. Then, what is left for it [consciousness]?

Having explained everything by these processes in which, at no time, were we obliged to have consciousness intervene, the fact of becoming conscious can no longer be for Freud, only a simple *quality*.

"What role, then, in our conception, does consciousness play, formerly so powerful and which covered and hid all other phenomena? It is nothing more than an organ of the senses which permits one to perceive the psychic qualities . . ." (602).

The analogy is pushed to the limit:

> We can see that the perception by our sense organs results in directing an occupation of attention toward the paths where the sensorial excitation expands; the qualitative excitation of the perceptive system helps to regularize the output of the mobile quantity in the psychic apparatus. We can attribute the same function to the superior sensorial organ of consciousness. By perceiving new qualities, it directs and distributes the mobile quantities of occupation. (603)

VII

A new world emerges from these explanations: the universe of the *psychic*. It has, indeed, a form of existence other than the one proper to the outside world, but it is, however, real and outside of consciousness. Just as sensitive perception reveals to us the outside world of matter, so also does the superior perception of consciousness reveal the outside world of the psychic. But just as the senses are limited in number, consciousness also has but few *receptors*. For "the processes of the systems, including those of the preconscious, lack psychic qualities, which is why they can appear as an object to consciousness only to the extent to which they lend themselves to its perception of the pleasant or of the unpleasant" (565). But this is only true for thought, for consciousness has everything it needs to receive the sensations.

> But during evolution, to obtain more delicate activities, it was necessary to render the progression of the representations more independent

of the signs of the unpleasant. The preconscious system had to have proper qualities which could attract consciousness; it probably acquired them by reconnecting these processes to the system of the memories of the signs of the language which was, for him, furnished with qualities. Thanks to the qualities of this system, consciousness, which until now had only the organ of sense of perceptions, became also the organ of sense of a part of our processes of thought. It had, from then on, in some way, two sensorial areas, one turned toward perception, the other toward the unconscious processes of thought. (565)[7]

That is why there exists a whole psychic world with a *becoming*, of *sui generis* "processes," of which consciousness only perceives a little. And that is why, for Freud, psychology leads us to a metapsychology, just as the expansion of the problem of perception in a certain direction leads to metaphysics.

And here, too, is the psychic device, ingenious and amazing. But there is a problem: it is condemned to inertia.

We have before us a succession of systems or a succession of *impersonal* processes, of processes in the third person: unconscious desires, preconscious elaborations, selective perception by consciousness; displacements of intensity and changes of occupation. . . . It would be nice if the system could function. But, it could do so only if there was, to take a term of comparison dear to Freud, a microscope. The light would show the different systems. It is desire that must play this role in the psychic apparatus. But, the psychic apparatus is not a material system; if it is apparatus, it is precisely psychic apparatus. For it to function, it needs the act of the "I," but this act precisely is excluded from the Freudian system.

Indeed, the unconscious desires are born and develop. They attach themselves to the preconscious formations; consciousness perceives them, but at no other time does an activity in the first person, *an act having a human form* and implying the "I," intervene. We could say the act of the "I" is precisely given by the desire. But it remains that this desire is submitted to transformations that are no longer acts of the "I." In any case, the systems that are too autonomous break the continuity of the "I," and the automatism of the processes of transformation and elaboration exclude its activity.

However, in spite of these criticisms that make the Freudian ideas unacceptable for concrete psychology, the chapter on "The Psychology of the Dream Processes" contains something very significant.

We are not talking about these modifications that Freud submits to classical notions that he has intervene in his works. But we must recognize that Freud, whatever his language, goes far beyond classical psychology. The latter, when it is about *mental processes*, only recognizes the association of ideas and its critique, on the one hand, and, on the other, what logic teaches us about intellectual functions. If we add to that the "fluid" models, in fashion at this time, we will have made the inventory of all the mental processes that psychology recognizes.

It is Freud who, for the first time, tried to introduce something new and precise in this area. He discovers a certain number of new processes which, whatever language is used, have a real signification, and with regression, displacement, and condensation, psychology at least leaves, for the first time, the common places of associationism, of logic and of dynamistic professions of faith.

But after doing this justice to Freud there is no reason to hide the fact that his theoretical works, such as they are today, are incompatible with this concrete psychology of which he is said to be the founder. Only, the demonstration of this perpetual conflict between the fundamental inspiration and the theoretical superstructure that characterizes the psychoanalysis of today is something completely different from the vulgar reproach of intellectualism. For the problem posed by Freud's errors goes beyond the domestic quarrels of classical psychology, and the procedures which are at the foundation of Freudian theories are not simply intellectualistic: they are common to a whole orientation of psychology to which intellectuals and their adversaries belong.

That is why we should not see, in the preceding analyses, the enumeration of Freud's personal errors. It would be arbitrarily limiting the bearing of our conclusions and losing the benefit of the teachings which come out of the Freudian speculations that we qualify as erroneous. For the errors in question derive from a necessity which goes beyond the order of magnitude of the individual deficiencies. Freud's theoretical attempt was inevitable: it was the first one to emerge after the discovery of the concrete point of view. And, besides, it was necessary, for the very comprehension of the essence of classical psychology, that the procedures of the latter be applied to facts which, issued from a diametrically opposed attitude, do not give them any grasp. For, as the reduction of the concrete facts of the abstract theories is purely verbal, we can only enumerate the models and the classical exigencies and offer up the list for critique.

We can, however, judge that we are burying the psychoanalytic theories too soon by seeking in them only a purely negative teaching, and that, from this point of view, our affirmations are not sufficiently supported by the preceding chapter. For everything we have shown until now is the contrast between the concrete and the abstract in the theories that we have examined, but, whatever this opposition, it is unquestionable that the facts discovered by Freud demand a psychological explanation. But if we take this point of view, we cannot hide the fact that all these facts orient us toward the *unconscious*. Thus we have one of two choices: either we yield to the facts to admit the unconscious, and the preceding critiques only concern the formulas and not the theories, and then being relative only to the *style*, they lose all their interest; or we claim that the critiques in question touch the very foundation and not simply the form, and then we must go all the way to the end and deny the unconscious, but with it the psychoanalytic facts which prove it, which would take away the benefit from all we have said about concrete psychology and, consequently, the right to any critique.

This is a dilemma the key to which is given by the idea that we have of the connections between the unconscious and psychoanalysis, and which expresses the worry created by our remarks. This worry cannot stand up to an attentive reading of this chapter and the dilemma appears fragile, but the gravity of the problem requires a frank explanation.

CHAPTER FOUR

The Hypothesis of the Unconscious and Concrete Psychology

We have shown in the preceding chapter the way in which Freud is led to introduce in the theory of the dream the hypothesis of the unconscious, and we have immediately indicated that this introduction results from the persistence, within the Freudian theory, of the exigencies and of the fundamental steps of abstract psychology. These indications could suffice to make one understand that the hypothesis of the unconscious does not mean for psychology this great conquest that we usually see, and that, besides, the novelty and the originality of psychoanalysis cannot reside in the discovery and in the exploration of the unconscious, since in a way, the unconscious represents in psychoanalysis only the measure of the abstraction that survives inside concrete psychology.

But it is enough to express these ideas for them to immediately provoke with psychologists a contradiction at least as violent as the ones that had provoked long ago the introduction of the unconscious. For, since the end of the nineteenth century, psychologists have gotten into the habit of considering the established place granted to the unconscious, as one of the most important victories of the new psychology, and it seems now, in favor of this conviction, that we could not abandon this notion without returning to the outworn ideas of intellectualist psychology.

To destroy ideas so deeply rooted in the mind of psychologists, the remarks of the preceding chapter are evidently not sufficient, considering that they constitute marginal notes on Freud's texts rather than a systematic analysis of the problem. It is therefore necessary to go back to the question to show in a methodical way, and independently from the step of Freud's ideas, the essential connection between the unconscious and the fundamental steps of abstract psychology.

But it is obvious, after what we have just said, that such a demonstration can be convincing only if it succeeds in showing, at the same time, that the condemnation of the unconscious does not mean the return to the affirmation of the exclusivity of consciousness. Without this, the threat of the return to this thesis of which psychologists have retained a very bad memory will still allow one to raise the previous question against all critique of the unconscious. The first part of the demonstration must be completed by a second one, having as an aim to show that *psychology is not enclosed between the two classical possibilities and that, consequently, the condemnation of the unconscious does not mean the return to consciousness.*

In truth, this requires only a single demonstration, for it is enough to show that the unconscious implies abstraction for the immediate result to be that concrete psychology finds itself placed, precisely by its concrete orientation, on a level where the classical opposition is of no more interest.

This is the theme of the present chapter. It is not about undertaking a complete examination of the problem of the unconscious; such an examination, which necessarily brings the problem of consciousness, would go beyond the framework of the present study.[1] That is why we approach the problem only in this particular aspect that we have just shown. Besides, while establishing that our critique of the unconscious raises very important problems for psychoanalysis, we are forced to resist the temptation of giving them a solution. The abandonment of the unconscious poses the problem of revision of fundamental notions of psychoanalysis — but the fact that we have to question the actual form of the classical notions as censorship and repression does not imply the need to offer a new solution. This is a matter for technicians, and they alone can know what the facts known to them can teach us, if we accept considering them from the concrete point of view. The critique should not and must not go beyond the demonstration of the necessity of this new orientation.

I

In favor of the prestige that the unconscious enjoys, psychologists willingly believe that, in the facts that are usually cited as proofs of the unconscious, the latter appears in such a direct and immediate way that it seems better to talk about *statement* rather than *hypothesis*. If it were so — if the unconscious were really a statement, or at least a hypothesis written in the facts themselves and consequently irresistible — we would evidently have nothing to say. And conversely, as long as this belief subsists, we can mistrust, with good reason, all critique of the unconscious. That is why it is important to show, by a review as general as possible, that there is between the facts, on the one hand, and the notion of the unconscious on the other, a distance great enough to make it possible to talk about *distortion* and to bring forth then the *problem of its legitimacy*. In other words, we must begin by rapidly showing that the facts cited as proofs of the unconscious are so, only because of a certain number of steps and exigencies which happen to be the ones that constitute the abstraction.

The starting point of the hypothesis of the unconscious is given by the fact that the account that the subject can give on his thought, on the one hand, and his complete thought *at the same time*, on the other hand, are not, in some cases, *equivalent*; in other words, the subject thinks more than he believes he thinks, and his admitted knowledge represents only a fragment of his true knowledge. The cases about which we make the most of the necessity of introducing the hypothesis of the unconscious are reduced to this general model, and when Freud talks about the unconscious when referring to the dream, he seems only to be showing its appropriateness. The subject knows more than he believes he knows; he declares at first that he does not know the meaning of the dream, whereas in the course of the analysis it is he who supplies all the elements necessary for his comprehension, and thus there is a gap between his *apparent knowledge* and his *true knowledge*; and as this true knowledge is a thought at the same level as the apparent knowledge, though it remains "hidden" to the subject, it seems right to admit with Freud a "modification of the terminology," and to say "instead of hidden, inaccessible . . ., by giving the exact description of the thing, inaccessible to the consciousness of the dreamer, or unconscious."[2]

Therefore, the unconscious seems to be in the case of the dream only a legitimate way of expressing an unquestionable fact. The fact is the contrast with the dreamer between apparent ignorance and "latent" knowledge concerning the meaning of his dream.

But how exactly did we establish this fact? First, we must describe the attitude of the subject toward his dream. The dreamer starts by giving a *descriptive story* of the dream; he tells of what he dreamed. He can later declare the dream as absurd or revolting, or he can find it "nice," but it is obvious that the meaning of the dream escapes him. Only, the ignorance we notice here is not a vague ignorance, as the one I can have before a text written in a language completely unknown to me, but a *determined* ignorance of something I could and should know, in short, the *ignorance of the latent content.*

And, indeed, the ignorance of the meaning of the dream by the dreamer acquires its signification only after analysis; its statement results only from the comparison of two stories, namely the story of the manifest content and the one of the latent content.

The manifest content shows me what there was in consciousness, and the latent content what there was, in reality, in the dream; in other words, the first one shows me the *conscious thought* of the subject, whereas the second one shows me his *whole thought.* The proposition that the subject ignores the meaning of the dream means then, that the subject ignores a thought that is truly his and that is "at this moment" in him, and this ignorance precisely proves that the whole thought is not conscious.

But we can see at the same time that the ignorance of the meaning of the dream by the dreamer proves the existence of the unconscious only if it is the *currently true* thought that goes beyond the *currently conscious* thought. But, the existence of this thought that goes beyond the manifest content of the dream is revealed to us only by the latent content, and the latter reveals a "thought" only to the extent to which we realized it.

Consequently, ignorance is a proof of the unconscious only when considered through realism; that is, solely because we do not consider it as pure and simple privation — for, in this case, it could not prove any presence under any form — but as relative to an absence that does not interest the whole psychic (system), but only the perpetual conscious mind. It must be understood that what is ignored still exists, but, as it is not conscious, it must be unconscious. Thus, the ignorance of the meaning of the dream by the dreamer is not, in itself, a proof of the unconscious, it becomes proof only indirectly and thanks to the realistic exigence.

It is the same for all the proofs of the latent unconscious quoted by Freud — for the unconscious memories and for the unconsciousness of the knowledge of hypnotized people. "Experience shows us . . .," says Freud,

> that a psychic element; that is, a representation, is not ordinarily conscious in a durable way. What is rather characteristic is the rapid disappearance of consciousness; the conscious representation of the moment is no longer so, the next moment, but can be again, under certain conditions that are easily achievable. In the meantime, I do not know what it was; we can say that it was *latent*, meaning that it was at each moment *capable of becoming conscious*. Similarly, by saying that is was *unconscious*, we give an exact description of the fact.[3]

It is clear that the availability of the memory proves a latent unconscious only if the memory is real before its conscious realization — that is, between the moment of its disappearance and the one when it reappears. Thus, its availability does not prove its latency *immediately*; it proves it only through realism, for the memories must survive their disappearance for us to be able then to say that their reappearance is only an actualization. In short, neither is the availability of the memories the *immediate proof* of a latent unconscious, since it only imposes this hypothesis thanks to the realistic exigence.

As for the unconscious with the hypnotized person, here is what Freud says:

> In the year 1889, in Nancy, when attending the singularly impressive demonstrations of Liebault and Bernheim, I was also a witness of the following experiment: a man who was in deep somnambulic state, and whom we had experienced in a hallucinatory way all that is possible, seemed, once awake, to ignore all the events of his hypnotic sleep. Bernheim summoned him to narrate what had happened to him during the hypnosis. The subject asserted he could not remember. But Bernheim insisted, he urged the man, assured him that he was able to remember, and then the man hesitated, started to take a hold of himself, first remembered obscurely one of the impressions that had been suggested to him, then another — the memory became

clearer and more complete, and finally appeared whole. But as this knowledge came to him only subsequently, and as he could not have learned it from any outside source, it is legitimate to conclude that he knew previously about these memories. Only, they were inaccessible to him, he did not know that he knew them and believed he did not know them. The situation is then exactly the same as the one we suppose in the case of the dreamer.[4]

There is, in other words, a gap between two successive attitudes of the subject, who first declares not knowing what he later remembers. Thus, it is evident that the subject is not deprived of the memory in question, since he is capable of remembering it and he ignores in fact only the extent of his knowledge: *thus, his ignorance compared to his knowledge proves the existence of the unconscious.*

But again, the ignorance in question is a proof of the unconscious only if the knowledge, which the subject only has in the second attitude, was already *real* in the first one; thus the ignorance does not reveal a pure and simple absence, but a relative absence, absence of consciousness and presence in the unconscious, and it is again through realism that the ignorance of the hypnotized person becomes a proof of the unconscious: *the story given in the second attitude played here the same role as the latent content in the case of the dream.*

The ignorance of the meaning of the dream by the dreamer, the availability of the memories, the disproportion between the apparent extent and the real extent of the posthypnotic memory are not proofs of the unconscious; they do not impose the unconscious *directly* and only make its introduction legitimate thanks to realism. The unconscious here is not *given* to us by the pure and simple facts, but by the *deformed* facts in the sense of one of the constitutive steps of classical psychology.

But psychoanalysts will tell us: whatever the truth be for the *latent unconscious*, it is not important, because if Freud talks about it, it is to show that the introduction of the notion of the unconscious already imposes itself with the examination of the facts independent of psychoanalysis. It concerns, on the one hand, preparing the mind of the reader for the broad use that psychoanalysis makes of this notion, and preventing us, on the other hand, from using it to raise, once more, the previous question against psychoanalytic facts. Besides, Freud expressly abandons the latent unconscious to the discussions of "philosophers." Indeed, immediately after the text about the availability of the memories, he says: "Philosophers will object, no doubt: no, the term unconscious has no signification here; as long as the representation was in the latent state, it was absolutely not psychic. If we wanted to contradict them on this point, we would get into a verbal fight in which we would have nothing to gain."[5] And the fact is that the latent unconscious is of little importance to the psychoanalyst: "It is by another path," says Freud, "always at the same place, that we reached the notion of the unconscious; that is, by the elaboration of facts where the psychic *dynamic* plays. . . ."[6]

II

"The experiment has revealed us," says Freud,

> that is, we have been forced to assume the existence of psychological processes or of very intense representations . . . which can have on mental life all the effects of the ordinary representations and even effects becoming, in turn, conscious under the form of representation, but which remain unconscious . . . It is here that the psychoanalytic theory intervenes to assert that representations of this kind cannot be conscious, because a certain force opposes it, that without it, they could become conscious and that we could see then, how little they differ from other psychic elements, recognized as such. This theory becomes irrefutable by the very fact that the psychoanalytic technique gave us the means to conquer the force of resistance and to render the representations in question conscious. The state where the representations are found before they are made conscious, we label *repression*, and the force that produced the repression and which maintained it, presents itself during the analytic work as *resistance*.
> Our conception of the unconscious derives from the theory of repression. It is the repressed person who is for us the model of the unconscious.[7]

The properly psychoanalytic unconscious is therefore not this unconscious that is only a shadow that is, the latent unconscious, but the living, acting, in a word, the dynamic unconscious that we are forced to admit, considering the fact of resistance and repression.

Here is how the argument is usually articulated: The starting point is given by resistance. During the analysis the subject resists certain thoughts. He forbids himself from having homosexual or incestuous desires whereas their presence results from the dream. We must notice right away that it does not concern simply *avoiding the public confession of a thing we know*, for, true resistance is previous to the knowledge: *the subject clearly resists before the knowledge*, he does everything not to have the analysis direct him to it: he starts by saying that nothing comes to his mind, later objects to the psychoanalytic method, finds it farfetched, etc., but as all this takes place before the appearance of a thought or a painful memory, it is legitimate to see the resistance. Then everything happens, "says" Freud, *as if the subject wanted to close off the entrance of consciousness to a condemned representation.* The resistance during the analysis reveals the existence of a force that refuses the entrance of consciousness to certain psychic states. But there is no reason to suppose that the resistance is something improvised, since the condemnation of the psychic state which we resist is previous to the analysis, considering that it results either from a value judgment of social origin, or from individual events previous to the analysis. In these conditions, the resistance during the analysis is only the manifestation of a resistance that bears on the whole of life in a continual way, which, in one phrase, is a *constant force*.

Thus, the representations we resist are real even as resistance stops them from acceding to consciousness. The first proof is that "we have found in the psychoanalytic technique the means to conquer the force of resistance and to make the representations in question conscious."[8] Freud even says that this is how the theory that asserts the existence of these representations, on the other side of resistance, so to speak, becomes "irrefutable" (11). But it is obvious that if this were all, we would simply be brought back to a distortion similar to the one which brings the latent unconscious. In fact, the most serious proof is that on the other side of resistance, the *existence of the representations in question is revealed by their action.*

The real proof of the unconscious resides in the fact that psychological states which are not conscious have conscious effects, whereas the real effect requires a real cause, and that is why it is necessary to introduce the notion of the unconscious.

The unconscious that can be *experimentally* proven is the dynamic unconscious. The latent unconscious will then profit from the truth of the dynamic unconscious, but it is true that we reverse this true order only for pedagogical reasons.

This time we would find ourselves confronted with a fact or a group of facts of which the observation itself is independent from the hypothesis that we want to prove through them, and we would attend the empirical genesis of the notion of the unconscious: our previous affirmations, valid for the *latent* unconscious, would no longer be so for the *dynamic* unconscious.

But this is not true. The fact cited as proof of the dynamic unconscious behaves like the proofs of the latent unconscious: it proves the unconscious only thanks to the realistic exigence.

Indeed, what does the proposition mean, after which a representation — in itself unconscious — can have conscious effects?

Let us take a concrete example. In the dream of the injection given to Irma, "Irma has a sore throat" means "I wish [there to be] an error of diagnosis." Thus, there is at first "explanation" only on the plan of the significations, since we are confronted with an explanation of text or, rather, the analysis of a dramatic scene. The desire of the error of diagnosis *explains*, then, the sore throat, as the Latin term *pater* explains the French term *pere*, or rather, as jealousy explains Othello's gesture. For the translation to become a relation of cause to effect, we must *realize* both contents. Then, "sore throat" will become "image" and "error of diagnosis," representation, and the fact that it is the meaning of the "representation" which demands the presence of the "image" will be translated on the "ontological" plan by making of the first, the *cause* and of the second, the *effect*.

Thus, the proof of the dynamic unconscious results essentially from the comparison of the manifest content and of the latent content. What we can positively see is that a significative intention has been represented by an unforeseen sign and that its adequate sign is of a different nature. As long as we remain on the level of the signification, this statement does not prove the unconscious. Consequently, the affirmation that a representation in itself unconscious has conscious effects is only the transposition in *ontological* terms of the fact that the second story gives *representation* for the adequate sign of the sense of one or several elements of the dream.

It is once that it is understood that the *linguistic* or *scenic* relation must immediately be changed into causal relation, and the latent content exist as really as the manifest content, that the inadequacy of the elements of the dream to the significative intentions of the latter will become a revelation of the existence in the psychic beyond of a representation.

In general, it is only the *realistic exigence* that transforms the facts into proof of the unconscious, whether it is a question of memory, hypnosis, or psychoanalytic facts.

To realism, however, we must add *functional formalism.*[9] For if the realistic exigence can seem natural to the point where we have the impression, by introducing the notion of the unconscious, of only obeying the facts, it is that these are already presented in such a way that starting from this presentation, the realistic procedure and, consequently, the hypothesis of the unconscious seem inevitable.

It is thus that, if the notion of censorship seems so plausible, it is because we immediately present the fact of resistance *in terms of a second story.* The subject has enormous difficulty in getting close to certain themes that later are found to be essentially significative. After making some "associations," he starts by saying that nothing comes to his mind, that he has nothing else to say. If we insist, he will say that he just had a few ideas, but they are not really important. If we further insist, he smiles haughtily and starts a discussion about psychoanalysis. He tries to baffle the analyst by saying, for example, that he will obviously be told that all this is resistance, but that those are only arbitrary assertions, etc. If we succeed in having him decide to find out, along with the analyst, if all this is really resistance and to continue his associations to that aim, we will finally see an idea appear that the subject really admits in a painful way that, for example, he has an incestuous desire, very clearly characterized, etc.

Here is the fact of resistance. What we have here is a story containing materials that shed light on the attitude of the subject. By saying that, we still have not left the level of significations and we have not stated any hypothesis. Only, instead of staying with the *signification*, realism seeks a *psychic entity to be realized*; we then say that the subject resisted the idea of incest, and the second story immediately states: resistance to a *representation*. It is from this fact thus presented that all psychological speculations will later start.

Formalism immediately replaces the personal drama by a drama in the third person where the actors are the *elements*; the whole drama is lowered to the level of these latter ones, and the fact is finally stated in the following way: the entrance to consciousness is refused to a representation.

As the subject resists the representations that explain the meaning of the dream, we can say that the scene which was played during the making of the dream is exactly the same one — that there, too, the representations showed up at the door of consciousness, but that they were refused. And we find ourselves led by the simple unfolding of formalism to the notion of censorship and, with it, to all the Freudian mythology of processes and instances.

It is therefore clear that to present it in the form of a *resistance to a representation*, we must give resistance, such as it can be described on the plan of daily statements, a formal description, and to convert with the help of this description the *significations* into *psychic entities*, and to transform the materials that shed light on the attitude of the subject into a small drama with a mechanical model.

But this manner of conceiving resistance somehow unbalances the fact itself. For the realism associated with formalism forces Freud to stress the *terms* of the story instead of its signification and to see in them the real *dynamic* factor, whereas, in reality, this dynamic factor is found elsewhere. And so the *Freudian description of resistance is not a statement, but already a hypothesis*, and as such it can be and should be criticized. Indeed, to say the subject found it difficult to admit that he had incestuous thoughts, and to say that he resisted the idea of incest, is not at all the same thing, for it concerns, in the first case, a simple "human" statement, and in the second one, a *psychological* description implying realism and the formal point of view.

III

We wanted to show, by this general review of the facts quoted by Freud as proofs of the unconscious, that if the facts in question bring in the unconscious, it is only because of a distortion due to the association of realism and formalism. It immediately follows that it is not the facts themselves, such as they can be established "in a human way," which produce the hypothesis of the unconscious, but an interpretation of these facts consistent with the point of view of abstraction.

This statement, which poses the legitimacy of a critique of the unconscious, still does not give us any information about its *genesis*. Thus, the development of the abstraction ends up at the unconscious only in certain determined cases. It is thus necessary to show precisely how realism arrives at producing the hypothesis of the unconscious.

We have seen that the first act of realism is the transformation of the significative story into an ensemble of psychological realities. This realization accomplished, the story is immobilized, in that its significative value is no longer at stake and that it simply becomes the starting point of a second story made in the spirit of functional formalism.

There is here, as I explained earlier, a *dividing of the significative story*: we extend the level of significations to another level, that of the psychic entities. We have indicated at the same time that the dividing has brought nothing new. Whether the story is still significative or already immobilized or divided, the only positive theme is still only the signification: the illusion that the dividing gives something new comes exclusively from the fact that once this is accomplished, the terms of the significative story become the themes of a new story, which is the *second story*.

Thus, precisely because in spite of the dividing the only real theme is established by the significative story itself, and because we just go around these terms, nothing stops us from coming back from the entities to the significations — that is, abandoning the dialectic of the second story to take back that of the significative story. We then have the impression of describing realities that remain constantly *present* during analysis, and which we examine. We express this fact by saying that the psychological entities in question are *conscious*.

And so, as we are in the presence of a pure and simple dividing, the affirmation that such and such a psychological fact is *conscious* only means that realism has worked on a story effectively given by the subject.

In other words, to say that a psychological fact is *conscious* is only the realistic translation of the fact that the subject has effectively made a determined story at the moment where the realization took place.

If realism could, on the one hand, be satisfied with only realizing the story effectively given by the subject, and accomplishing, on the other, the realization as we just indicated, the problem of the unconscious would never be posed. But it happens that in some cases, realism has to *dissociate the pairing* established by the significative story and its *ontological* double and, in other cases, to *postulate a story* that has not been effectively given by the subject.

The first case is given when the ontological double must be realized not only apart from, but also previous to the story itself. It is what happens in the latent unconscious. The memories that constitute the materials of the story that I am now telling are not the only ones I can have. I can suddenly stop and think of the trip I just took. Other memories will then appear. In the same way, I can take other attitudes, implying memories which constitute the matter of very different stories. But for now I do not realize all these stories; in other words, only one group of memories is current, the others are just *available*. Classical psychology calls on the notion of latency to explain this availability. But as we are on the level of realistic conceptions, we must realize the memories in question, as if the stories were happening, but as they are not so, we will have to put the ontological double of the story apart from the story itself. It will then, of course, be impossible to realize this movement of coming and going between significations and entities, which becomes possible when realism works on a story that has in fact been told; it will be impossible to return at will to the dialectics of the story itself; the result of the realization will be given, but the real aspect of the psychological fact will be lacking, since there was no story. It is this fact, that in the absence of the story we had nevertheless to realize it, that we translate with the notion of latent unconscious.

This can be illustrated by examples other than the latency of memories. In the posthypnotic memory, also, it is about realizing a story at a moment when it is not yet effective. The subject is at first incapable of reporting what happened during hypnosis; he can, however, on the pressing injunctions of the hypnotist, remember the essential. From this we conclude that he knew something at the very moment when he asserted not knowing anything, thus, the necessity of realizing the story previously to its reality, and we then end up with the hypothesis of *unconscious knowledge.*

Thus, realism finds itself led in the case of the latent unconscious to talk only about the second of the two terms that it presents when working on an effective story, the one that results from the dividing. But as realism is an arbitrary procedure, the psychological entities that must represent the ontological doubles of significations are entirely *fictitious.* This fictitious character of the ontological level cannot appear when two levels coexist, for it is exactly the effective presence of the signification which is interpreted as the presence of psychological entities. But when, in order to explain the availability of the memories, for example, we are led to set aside the fictitious term, realism prevents psychologists from noticing the fiction, which then appears as *unconsciousness,* transposed consistently with realism. In short, *the term unconscious is only the translation of the fact that we are concerned with purely fictitious psychological entities.*

It is the same for the dynamic unconscious, even though the functioning of realism is, in this case, different from what we have just seen.

The unconscious is not brought here by *the necessity of realizing the ontological double of the story before the story itself,* but by the fact that we are brought *to postulate a story that has not effectively been given by the subject.*

Let us take the example of the dream. The dream has two contents: a manifest content and a latent content. To be more exact, the dream only has one content: for it results precisely from the analysis that the terms of the story regarding the dream do not have their conventional significations, but another signification that can be determined only by the analysis, and the impression that the dream has two contents uniquely results from the fact that we can try conventional dialectic with regard to the dream that is, as we know, ineffective in most cases.

The result of the analysis is that the dream establishes a story that is not the one it should have been *if the significative intentions had used their adequate signs.* Consequently, the story of the dream such as it is given by the subject, and where the significative intentions are *disguised,* must be replaced by another one where the latter appear with their *adequate* signs.

As far as realism is concerned, the question is then asked in the following way. First of all, there is no question that the manifest story of the dream must be realized, since the dream effectively took place. But then, we must also realize the latent content, since it gives the true thought of the dream. And finally these two realizations must take place simultaneously, since the dream, even though the subject only knows the manifest content, already has the signification that the analysis will later update. *We thus find ourselves under the obligation of having to realize a story that is not effective at the moment where it must be realized.* And we find again the model that we already know: considering that what is missing is precisely what can guarantee the reality of the ontological double and that can give the illusion of moving among truly existing psychological facts, that is the effective story, we will once again have to speak of *unconscious phenomena.*

In short, the introduction of the unconscious in the theory of the dream results from the fact that parallel to the effective story, we feel obliged to realize another story that is not effective, but which we postulate in the name of this statement that the true thought of the dream demands a story different from the manifest story.

And as it often happens that nothing corresponds in the manifest story to the latent story, the entities that will result from the dividing of the latter can evidently only be *unconscious.* It is so, for example, that "Irma has a sore throat" means, in the "Dream of the Injection Given to Irma," "I hope there is a diagnostic error." This desire is not mentioned in the dream; thus, if it is realized, it will be only under the form of an unconscious desire.

IV

That the latent unconscious, like the dynamic unconscious, results from the realization of stories, I think there can be no doubt. For, on the one hand, the memories that are really available can be revealed to us only by the stories that actually took place, and it is from these stories that we later go back, by a fiction of which the mechanism is clear, to where we suppose them to be nonexistent, to assert their *latency* as an *afterthought.* The meaning of the dream, on the other hand, can be known only when the analysis has allowed giving the story latent content. And not only do we go *backward* to realize the story, but again we go from there to explain the genesis of the dream. But, in this explanation the base of reference still remains the story of the latent content, and all the problems that Freud poses in the *Traumdeutung* about the elaboration of the dream result from a simple comparison between the *text* of the latent content and that of the manifest content. Thus it is that the very duality of the story reveals first the *disguising* and the *censorship*; that a first comparison made from the point of view of the presentation of the motives shows the condensation; and that the same comparison, but made in the formal point of view, poses the problem of regression, etc.

It is also clear that the dynamic unconscious results from the realization of a postulated story. And the true problem does not consist then in knowing whether there has been any realization of the story or not, but in knowing if this realization is justified.

If we look closely, the latent content is nothing other than the dream such as it would have been if, instead of being dreamed, it had simply been "thought." The manifest content is *symbolic*, the significative intentions do not appear in it with their adequate signs, whereas the latent content is the same text, but deciphered; that is, giving the same significative intentions, but with their adequate signs. Thus, the aim of the analysis, according to Freud, is to redo in a reverse sense the work of the dream; that is, *to go from the manifest content to the latent content*. It is clear, consequently, that this conception of the analysis comes back retroactively to pose to the dream a conventional thought expressing the meaning of the dream by giving their adequate signs to the significative intentions; this thought was then distorted for reasons that Freud tries to indicate with much ingenuity. We are then in the presence of a real postulate, *the postulate of the priority of the conventional thought*.

It is this postulate alone that explains why Freud feels he has to realize, previous to the manifest story, the deciphered signification of one of its terms, and that he has to postulate a story that had not effectively taken place; and, as without this necessity, we do not end up at the dynamic unconscious, we rediscover at the base of this notion the postulate of the priority of the conventional thought that consists of the motive force of realism when it ends up at the unconscious.

The big problem is therefore the one that consists in knowing whether the postulate in question is legitimate or not. Freudians can essentially come up with two kinds of proofs. We can first say that the essential difference between the thought of the day before and the dream is that the dream is symbolic, whereas the thought of the dream is not. We must therefore explain this change of attitude and we can, later, purely and simply, doubt that what we realize is precisely the conventional story of the thought of the dream, and say that we only realize the *dynamic* factors, which act in the dream without appearing in it, as, for example, the memories of childhood which the subject used in the dream but ignores.

As for the first argument, it effectively states what is striking at first in the dream. Why is it that, confronted by a psychological formation, we suddenly have to resort to analysis instead of keeping the attitude that we usually have with the stories? Why are desires expressed by the dream not mentioned as they usually are, or why is analysis necessary to understand them? Is it not precisely the proof of the fact that the ordinary thought was *disguised*? And then, we feel forced to assume at the heart of the symbol its true signification and to then go back to the original text. We can add that the subject himself ignores this true signification, that he can only do it when the resistance is conquered and the repression is stopped, and we will be forced to recognize *the necessity of posing the dynamic unconscious.*

It is obvious that the main argument consists of the model of the translation. The dream is the original text that, considering censorship and repression, can only appear through a symbolic translation. But we forget one thing: it is not absolutely necessary to conceive all symbolism according to the model of translation. It is perhaps legitimate under the form of translation and of disguise, to conceive the *voluntary and reasoned symbolism.* It is thus that we want to represent "ideas" or "feelings" by painting or by music. There, we effectively go from the adequate sign to the symbol. But to say that the dream proceeds exactly in the same way, except that the adequate sign is unconscious, may be a somewhat hasty affirmation. For whatever may be the question of the unconscious, what is certain, is that the dream does not result from a desired and reasoned symbolism. The proof is that the subject ignores not only the signification of the symbols of the dream, but also that there is a symbol in general, and that, the psychologists themselves had ignored until the arrival of psychoanalysis. It may not be impossible that the symbolism of the dream is, under these conditions, of a completely different nature.

If we consider the dream as the realization of a desire, it essentially appears to us as a *scenario*. The scenario has for *form* precisely the desire in question; the dream follows, so to speak, the dialectics of this desire. It is the same if we consider that the dream reproduces, with recent materials, infantile settings. Thus, for the arrangement of a certain number of elements, consistent with the scenario of a desire, or with an infantile setting, to take place, it is not necessary that the desire or the setting in question be, previous to the dream itself, the object of a distinct representation for the subject, as it is not necessary to think that during a tennis match the rules of the game act *unconsciously*. It is useless, in the same way, to attribute to the desire or the setting a *distinct psychological existence*. For this desire and this setting are released from the analysis of the story and represent results of abstractions. What is real is the signification of the story itself, and if we abide by this signification, we will not have any reason to realize apart and in the unconscious what is *implied* as dialectics in the setting of the dream.

In these conditions the symbolism of the dream is precisely not the "disguising of a primitive text." The fact is that its elements are caught in an unforeseen dialectics, an individual dialectics that must be analyzed, and the analysis must show us what this dialectics is and what the form or the setting that explains the dream is, but not try to go back to "I-do-not-know-which *original text*."

We are in the presence of two hypotheses. One, the Freudian hypothesis, conceives of the dream as a true transposition starting from an original text that the work of the dream distorts; for the other one, on the contrary, the dream is the result of the functioning of an individual dialectic. The essential difference between these two conceptions resides in the fact that in the first one the dream is something derived, whereas in the second one, it is the main phenomenon and is self-sufficient. In these conditions the dream does not have, properly speaking, two contents — manifest and latent. It can have a manifest content only if we try to interpret it on the plan of conventional dialectics. In point of fact, these dialectics, however, are ineffective in the case of the dream: the dream is not their work, since it can only be explained by a personal dialectics. The dream then has only one content, the one that Freud calls the latent content. But this content, the dream has immediately, and not subsequently to a disguise. The symbolism appears to be a disguise *only if we replace the dialectics that explains the dream by its story and if we realize this story previous to the dream itself.* Consequently, for the necessity of the realization of the latent content previous to the manifest content to be evident, we must give a static interpretation of the form of the dream; that is, to *abandon the signification* and to *realize the story.* It is thus, for example, that dreams are often explained by a childhood memory. But instead of conceiving this childhood memory from a truly dynamic standpoint, that is, as the sign of a setting or a behavior, we consider it from a static standpoint, by making it the memory that we realize as a thing and that we will be obliged later to endow with properties and mechanical effects.

Thus it is that the necessity of introducing the unconscious can be explained. If we interpret the childhood memory in the dynamic point of view as meaning a behavior or a setting, we cannot say it is absent from the dream: it is present like the rules of the game are present in a tennis match. But if we interpret it from the static standpoint, as memory-representation or memory-image, therefore as a psychological entity, it then needs a separate place, and since it is not statically present in the dream, we will have to project it into the unconscious.

In this way, the facts on which rests the argument that we are considering cannot prove the legitimacy of the postulate of the priority of conventional thought, because, in reality, this postulate is previous to these facts. The symbolism of the dream can prove this postulate only if we clearly conceive this symbolism as a disguise, as a transposition, but this assumes a conception of the elaboration of the dream that has as a base of reference the realized story of the latent content, which precisely implies the postulate in question.

It is the same for the second group of arguments. We saw earlier that Freud insists on the fact that the psychoanalytic unconscious is the dynamic unconscious that reveals its existence by a real action in consciousness, and that the theory becomes irrefutable by the fact that, once resistance is lifted, the unconscious elements become conscious.

As for the first part of the argument, the fundamental fact on which it rests is essentially the action of childhood memories.

It is easy to show, after what we have just said, that it is because of a disguise, or rather an illusion, that we can say that when we have found the explanation of a dream in a childhood memory, we have really found an "unconscious factor producing conscious effects."

What do we mean exactly when we assert that this childhood memory explains that dream? It essentially means showing that at the base of the dream in question can once again be found a setting that constitutes the signification of a childhood memory. But the result of this observation is that the setting that is at the base of the childhood memory is *present* in the dream; consequently, the appearance of the memory does not bring the revelation of a psychological reality distinct from the dream itself, but simply allows the identification of the setting actually present in the dream such as it is. In other words, by owning the memory in question, we did not tear out the veil that covered an entity, but we have obtained a new light, a decisive piece of information on the problem with which we are concerned. It is not our vision that has gone from one reality to another, but our comprehension has been expanded with the help of a new version. If we go along on the level of abstraction, we begin by fulfilling the manifest dream; we will later realize the childhood memory that appeared, and we will do something with it, in such a way that the memory which before was only an *instrument of recognition*, will become the *revelation of a thing*. We will then have to, on the one hand, create a mechanical scheme to explain its action and, on the other, speak of the return to consciousness of a factor that had acted unconsciously.

We cannot therefore interpret facts of this kind as the revelation of an actually acting unconscious. And again the postulate, intimately tied to realism, precedes the facts which justify it.

The analysis proving the postulate of the priority of conventional thought leads us to a conclusion similar to the one that we obtained by the examination of the proofs of unconscious.

The facts that we cite as proofs of this postulate are indeed only the distorted facts consistent with the latter.

The first distortion of facts consists in the very manner in which we conceive the role of analysis. In the minds of Freud and Freudians, analysis is essentially a reconstitution, even though Freud recognizes that all the moments of the analysis do not have a historic value. Thus, the fact, such as it is stated, is that analysis teaches the subject what he previously ignored, as, for example, the meaning of the dream.

But, one might say, it is the subject who dreamed and it is he who supplied the elements necessary for the interpretation; thus, he *knows*, and as this knowledge is obviously not available, he knows, but in an unconscious way. Thus, this is just another distortion to which the fact is submitted. The subject asserts not knowing the meaning of the dream. We do not want to accept this affirmation, and we say that the subject knows. And we do not believe that the subject does not know, precisely because we assume the story of the latent content as being realized, and once again, it is not the facts that prove the postulate, but it is in the name of the postulate that we distort the facts.

This statement is not surprising at all. Once it is established that the postulate in question is intimately tied to realism and to abstraction in general, it is natural that we recognize in it, not as an empirical statement, but as an *a priori* principle. And it would have been absolutely useless to insist on this point if psychoanalysts had not gotten into the habit of presenting the unconscious as a hypothesis that the facts *immediately* impose on us.

V

Now that it appears to be established that we are confronted with a postulate in the real sense of the word, it is fitting to examine the nature of this postulate, with a little bit more precision than we have done until now.

It is obvious that if the dream, and in general the neurotic symptoms, have a meaning, they have this meaning at the time they are being produced; and if the dream in particular is the satisfaction of a desire, it is this satisfaction at the moment it is dreamed. Thus, in this point of view, the analysis only expresses what the dream *is* and what the neurotic symptoms *are*, and as this explanation is essentially taking place on the level of the story, we can say that in this determined sense the analysis makes the being in the first person go to the level of the story, and from this point of view the *latent content* of a dream or of a neurotic symptom is nothing else but a *description*; that is, a *conventional story of which the theme is a lived attitude*. If analysis is necessary, it is that the story of the dream such as it is created by the subject is not an exhaustive account of what has been lived, and if we look closely, the manifest content of the dream only contains the "scenic" setting of the actually lived attitude; the mystery of the dream is made in large part by this inadequacy of the story to the real content of the attitude that constitutes it: the being in first person contains more than the available story. Thus, the postulate of the priority of the conventional thought, by setting the reality of the latent content, only corrects this state of things, in such a way that the gap between the being in the first person and the story disappears. For the latent content is nothing else but the adequate story of the lived attitude, and by realizing it to make of it the starting point of the explanation of the genesis and of the work of the dream, we only say in principle that there always should be an adequate story to the being in the first person. This is the true meaning of the postulate that we are examining. It essentially means that we say in theory that we cannot live more than we can think, that in other words, all behavior supposes an adequate story from which it proceeds. That is why when a behavior is more than the story accompanying it, we will project in the unconscious what lacks in the story to be adequate. The essence of this postulate is to say that the psychological fact can only exist in a narrative form, and by saying that the postulate of the conventional signification is only, in reality, *the postulate of the narrative thought*, we only stated its true essence.

It is not difficult to find, from the preceding remarks, the intellectualistic scheme at the base of the postulate that we are examining. For this idea that all behavior supposes an adequate story from which it proceeds asserts the primacy on the *being* of the *representation*, and that of the reflective attitude; that is, *descriptive*, on *life*. But, in reality, there is here only one consequence of this fact, that realism is still working on the *stories*, in spite of its protest and its attempts at finesse. The postulate itself represents nothing else but generalization, and, in some way, the absolute position of what we see in ordinary stories. *It is because the ordinary stories are effectively descriptive, and it is because it is with the help of descriptive stories that psychology accomplishes its first realizations and creates its fundamental entities, that we set up later this kind of psychological facts in universal kind, and that we postulate, where the adequate story is lacking, an adequate unconscious story.*

This is how the true function of the unconscious becomes clear. As it is the place of the stories postulated in the name of the exigence that we just described, its function is essentially to assure this exigence its permanent value. Indeed, we will speak of the unconscious precisely where the fact such as it is stated throws off the postulate. In this way, no matter what the fact lacks for the postulate to be valid, being always brought by the unconscious, the postulate becomes irrefutable and, by effect of a ricochet, the unconscious itself becomes equally irrefutable; the unconscious makes the postulate irrefutable, and the postulate makes the unconscious irrefutable.

VI

The first important conclusion of this analysis is that psychoanalysts are really wrong to believe that psychoanalysis and the unconscious are inseparable. It cannot be so, for the fundamental inspiration of psychoanalysis is orientation toward the concrete, whereas the unconscious is inseparable from the constitutive steps of abstract psychology. What could have created and maintained psychoanalysts' illusion on this point, is that psychoanalysis had to, and still has to, use the unconscious more than any other doctrine. It is an unquestionable fact, but it is not certain that the explanation is the one that Freud and Freudians give, namely that the facts themselves enforce the unconscious.

As the unconscious essentially measures the gap between the facts and the postulate of the narrative thought, we will have to resort to it, all the more so because the point of view where we stand will move away from the classic equation between the psychological facts and the narrative thought. This is precisely the case of psychoanalysis. To place ourselves in the concrete point of view, to accept as psychological facts only the segments of the life of the particular individual, to assign to psychological analysis as essential objective the establishing of the signification of the psychological fact in the whole of the life of the singular "I," always implies the transcending of the immediate stories, and the necessity of clarifying them with the themes of analysis, to determine the precise signification of the act of the "I." Psychoanalysis is therefore oriented by its fundamental inspiration toward the inadequacy between the immediate narrative thought and the true signification of the act lived by the subject. Thus, if we do not abandon the realistic exigence and, in general, the procedures of abstract psychology, we will be necessarily led to the notion of the unconscious, by the ways that we tried to describe. Thus, the unconscious necessarily appears in psychoanalysis, but this necessity is not an empirical one, but an *a priori* necessity and due to the fact that psychoanalysts use it in the elaboration of the facts of classical psychology.

We then witness this curious fact, if not paradoxical, that the true inspiration of psychoanalysis acts only in the beginning and in the discovery of the facts, to immediately stop at the time of the theoretical interpretation. And it is because at the time of the interpretation of the facts, the action of the concrete orientation stops to give way to the classical steps, that the unconscious appears. In one word, the unconscious appears at the time when the hypotheses adequate to concrete psychology should appear, and it follows that the dynamic unconscious, far from being a really interesting discovery of psychoanalysis, only shows its theoretical powerlessness.

It is true that Freud thought he could escape from many objections and even create a modern theory by expressing the hypothesis of the dynamic unconscious. It is one more misunderstanding to dispel, for it is evident at first sight that the unconscious of psychoanalysts is dynamic only in name, or rather that the dynamism of this unconscious can have no psychological signification.

Freud does not stop at what is really dynamic in the facts that he considers; that is, the *acts*, the *behaviors* and the *form*, or the law of the latter. He seeks instead *static* elements that he can establish. That is how he behaves concerning the childhood memories that psychoanalysis often talks about. The dynamic side of these memories, that is, the signs of their setting, is not forgotten: we showed it in the preceding chapter, and we also have to add that in the recent evolution of psychoanalysis, as we will see later, the true dynamism plays a larger and larger role. But as far as the fundamental realizations which end at the unconscious, everything happens as if we wanted to retain only the static aspect, and it is so that what is realized, is the memory-image or the memory-representation, and therefore an entity and not a setting or a form. From then on the dynamism is conceived only in the causal relation and in the emotionalism, and we only look for a small mechanical scheme where the memory-element realized, and reinforced by the emotional forces, acts as a thing. We thus end at a dynamism which is purely and simply copied from the physical dynamism.

But such a dynamism can have no psychological signification. For the only dynamism that can be psychologically conceived, is the dynamism of the "I;" that is, a dynamism in first person, and any conception that would give dynamism to the so-called psychological *elements* is necessarily mythological. It is so with the dynamic action of childhood memories, of their "attraction," and, in general, of all the actions that, according to Freud, they practice, precisely because they can have the properties attributed to them only if they are conceived as things; but, then, going on to the level of the third person, they stop being psychological.

Nothing is changed in this situation when we assert that the essence of the dynamic unconscious resides in emotionalism. For the emotional facts of which the Freudians fill the unconscious also result from realizations starting from the significative stories which have appeared during analysis, or have been given as latent content; they owe their birth to the classical steps. And, besides, to make of them the essence of the unconscious life, we must give them their own independent activity, but in this way, by having them go on the level of the third person, we can only end up with a vast mythology.

VII

The preceding analyses and reflections do not constitute a refutation of the hypothesis of the unconscious. They have another objective. They were essentially demonstrating two points, namely that the unconscious is inseparable from the fundamental procedures of abstract psychology and that, on the other hand, far from constituting progress in psychoanalysis, it clearly shows a regression; the abandonment of the concrete inspiration and the return to the classical steps.

This character of the unconscious stands out from what precedes with sufficient clarity; it is, meanwhile, useful to emphasize it by some additional remarks.

The use of the hypothesis of the unconscious represents such little progress that Freud commits the very mistakes he attributed to his adversaries.

We know that the fundamental reproach that Freud makes of classical theorists of the dream is that they have considered the dream as a negative phenomenon, as a group of ineffective and falsified operations. Freud is far from sharing this opinion, and we have shown how he succeeded in going beyond it. But beside this aspect of the Freudian theory where the dream is revealed essentially as "a psychological fact in the real sense of the word," it is impossible not to recognize a certain intervention of the classical conception, led by the use of the notion of the unconscious. This notion implies, as we have shown, the postulate of the priority of the conventional thought. In virtue of this postulate, all thought due to an individual dialectic will appear necessarily as *derived*, as explained from a thought that expresses *the same theme* in a *conventional* way, in a word, as *distorted and repressed conventional thought*. And that is why two problems will always be present: a first problem concerning the *meaning*, but also a second one concerning the *cause and the mechanism of this distortion*, and we know with what care and precision Freud tried to resolve them.

In any case, the dream is once again, in some way, ineffective, thus negative, though the causes of this defect are, with Freud, positive.

The dream cannot be self-sufficient and no psychological fact is self-sufficient, considering that what is important to psychology is its signification as a segment of individual life, and this signification can be determined only by a documentation supplied by the subject. But by asserting the insufficiency of the dream as it is given, by basing ourselves on this consideration, we would not fall back into the classical mistake. But we fall back into it precisely by considering the insufficiency of the dream, not only from the point of view of what is necessary to understand its complete sense, but relative to another psychological reality that contains the really important elements and on which our interest finally rests. The concrete point of view would have allowed bringing everything exclusively back to the dream, without considering it as something that should not have normally been what it is. But Freud could not use the concrete inspiration of his doctrine for the interpretation of the facts and, thanks to the postulate of the priority of conventional thought, had to bring into his theory the scheme of classical prejudice which he dislikes the most.

The second fundamental reproach that Freud makes of his predecessors, is their contending uniquely with the manifest content in the study of the dream, or, as we have said, with the postulate of the conventional signification.

But we already know that in the first phase of his thought, where he follows the concrete inspiration of psychoanalysis, Freud went beyond this point of view and ended in the discovery of individual dialectics, a discovery that is at the very base of concrete psychology. But if we examine his theoretical works, we will be forced to recognize that Freud has not abandoned the point of view of the manifest content as radically as his declarations could make us believe.

The hypothesis of the unconscious implies, as we have shown, the postulate of narrative thought. Consequently, the unconscious is introduced only because of the fact that the dream is disappointed with regard to the exigence expressed by the postulate in question; in other words, we have to introduce the unconscious only because we expected to find *everything* in the manifest content, and since everything is not in it, we feel that we have to *project the complement in the unconscious*. In this way, we *did not really abandon the manifest content* since it continues to remain the base of reference to situate the psychological facts.

We end up this way at a sort of *epistemological paradox:* here again, the explanation consists of the elimination of what is to be explained. The dream took place: an individual dialectics has functioned, unforeseen and unforeseeable ties have been established between significative intentions and signs: instead of taking their usual forms, thoughts took forms which ordinarily are reserved to other thoughts. The explanation, by introducing the unconscious and by displaying in it the conventional story postulated for the explanation of the dream, *makes the individual dialectics disappear*, and the most interesting fact finds itself eliminated; it is a conventional dialectics that has existed and still exists, but it can be found precisely in the unconscious.

And so we are finally brought back to the postulate of the conventional signification. For, the structure of the thought that is projected in the unconscious is such that the significations are attached to their adequate signs, and it is even to rediscover this adequacy that the dream does not respect that we introduce the unconscious, to realize the signs of its significations which, while being present in the dream, are represented by other signs.

We can reach similar conclusions by examining in the same way the third of the main reproaches that psychoanalysts give classical psychology. The model of every thought, according to the latter, is conscious thought. Freud asserts, on the contrary, having moved the emphasis from conscious to unconscious.

If we consider Freud's theoretical constructions, we must, however, recognize that in one way, Freud made the same mistake. For with Freud too, and this is made evident by what we have just said about the manifest content, it is consciousness which remains, in spite of the base of reference which allows one to situate the psychological facts. For if we did not expect that all the signification of a behavior be formulated into a story, that is, being conscious, we could not consider as an extraordinary discovery the fact that it is not always so. It is because of this disappointed exigence that the Freudians can admire their discovery of the unconscious. In this way Freud's theoretical constructions, far from dismissing the conscious, represent a vision relative to consciousness.

But consciousness does not only intervene in psychoanalysis as a *base of reference*, it also constitutes the model according to which the unconscious is made. The structure of the complement that we project in the unconscious is exactly copied on the conscious thought, and it is solely because, besides the act, we look for a story whose structure is the same as that of the stories which ordinarily accompanies the actions, that we have to postulate the unconscious. That we are then told of the original processes of the unconscious, of its states that we may never know exactly, does not change the truth of our affirmation, since there are here only progressive refinements which Freud has brought to an edifice of which the substructures have been elaborated in accordance with conscious thought.

VIII

It seems then unquestionable that the unconscious is indissolubly tied to the fundamental steps of abstract psychology, to the point where it brings Freud back to the prejudices that he precisely claims to fight. In this way, the falsehood of this hypothesis is indirectly demonstrated. For, tied to classical steps, it rests like them on the point of view of the third person. We could stop the examination of the problem of the unconscious now, since it suffices to show from a step or from a notion that it implies abstraction for it to be no longer in question in concrete psychology. But the classical steps are so rooted in us that the hypothesis of the unconscious seems to be an easy and convenient hypothesis, even irresistible, and we do not notice that this ease and this convenience come exclusively from the fact that we forget the fundamental absurdity. It is no longer useless then, in these conditions, to go to the direct demonstration of this absurdity, even though this demonstration cannot bring in the debate any really essential element, considering that the hypothesis of the unconscious will find itself eliminated only by the new orientation of psychology. But precisely for this reason we will contend with a rapid demonstration.

Psychological themes can only be known by the story. When a certain story appears to psychologists as the description of *sui generis* realities, it is no longer an *immediate theme*, but an *interpretation*, and the immediate theme can only be the *signification*; everything else is just hypothesis. Whatever the protests of the introspectionist psychologists, they also only filter the themes of the significative stories through a complicated device of hypotheses and of postulates.[10]

If we end up at the unconscious, it is because not being able to be satisfied with the effective story, we have to postulate stories which do not take place at the time that they are fulfilled, and are created consistently with a group of principles which are far from being summaries of experience. In some way, we substitute ourselves for the subject so as to give, in accordance with certain exigencies, a story that the subject did not give, and it is to lend him these stories created simply in the name of purely theoretical exigencies that we introduce the unconscious. And so we can say without paradox that since the unconscious is the place of postulated but nonexistent stories, the unconscious phenomena represent psychological facts created entirely "for the needs of the cause."

The falsehood of the unconscious is shown by the fact that the phenomena alleged to be unconscious are entirely in the air. For if it is true that there exists no real psychological theme other than the effective story, the unconscious that results from the realization of stories which did not take place cannot correspond to any reality; for the hypothesis of the unconscious, this is an impossible impasse to get out of.

IX

This conclusion of the preceding analyses, namely that the unconscious is neither imposed by the facts themselves, nor maintainable in the presence of reflection sufficiently clear on the nature of the psychological facts, does not at all mean that we must return to the exclusivity of consciousness, and the affirmation that concrete psychology must turn away from the hypothesis of the unconscious does not announce the return from antithesis to thesis.

Far from that, it is enough to consider this intimate[11] relation between the notion of consciousness, on one hand, and the realistic attitude, on the other, to understand that in the point of view of a psychology that turns away from *realities* to study only the *dramatic significations*, the classical problem of consciousness is an infinitely remote problem, and that the true solution can be represented by neither one of the two classical theses, for it is found on a level where the classical antithesis has no interest, nor any signification.

However, the complete demonstration of the incompatibility between concrete psychology and the thesis of the exclusivity of consciousness would go far beyond the frame of the present study. For, even a superficial inspection of the implications of this problem clearly shows that such a demonstration means a general examination of the notion of consciousness. But it would not be prudent to compromise the importance of a certain number of ideas, valid in themselves, by a development which can figure in this study only on the second level.

Besides, the natural movement of our analyses does not take us to this general demonstration. What we have shown is that only the procedures of the abstraction allow us to assert the unconscious with regard to the psychoanalytic facts. Under these conditions, to separate the reproach of "reaction" from our critique, it will be enough to show that to deny the unconscious about these facts does not mean that we have to find the way in which the content of the Freudian unconscious can be conceived as conscious.

The negation of the unconscious character of a psychological fact would imply the affirmation of its conscious character only if it were absolutely necessary to conceive in one way or another the reality of the fact in question. In this way, for example, the negation of the unconscious character of the latent content of the dream would imply its position in consciousness only if the latent content had to be conceived absolutely as psychologically real at the moment when the dream developed and unfolded.

It is unquestionable that the feeling of this necessity exists with psychologists. They are convinced, indeed, that if the generative representation of the dream is not unconscious, it must be conscious in one way or another. This feeling, for example, corresponds to the thesis according to which the facts that Freud calls unconscious, participate, also, in consciousness, though in a weaker way than the facts of clear consciousness: Freud quotes and refutes this thesis in the beginning of his recent work, *Das Ich und das Es* (p. 13 ff).

It is also obvious that this feeling is valid only if it is established that we have to conceive the facts in question as psychologically real.

We already know that the content of the unconscious results from the realization of the latent content. The latter is only the explicit story of the meaning of the dream, which is postulated for the subject as being unconscious latent content. But the negation of the unconscious can bring the affirmation of consciousness of the latent content only if we continue to postulate the reality of the latent content, that is, if we continue to require from the subject, as from the dream, the explicit story of the meaning of the dream — that is, the dream as well as *the knowledge of the meaning of the dream.* We find thus at the base of this necessity, which appears so imperious, *the postulate of the narrative thought* — that is, the same confusion between the *being* and the *knowing* that we already have recorded about the unconscious.

In these conditions, the condemnation of the unconscious makes us in one way or another, place in consciousness the facts that we refuse to consider as unconscious only if the negation bears uniquely on the *character* or the *way of being* of a certain number of facts of which we already recognize the reality. It is what precisely characterizes the position of the thesis that we just cited.

Our critique is of another nature. *We put the negation on the very reality of allegedly unconscious facts.* Indeed, these facts appear to us as entirely fabricated, consistent with exigencies that are not only incompatible with the orientation of concrete psychology, but also with the facts themselves, considering that they comprise a continual distortion of the latter.

It does not seem right to require from the subject anything else than the accomplishment of the act. The signification of the act can be known to the subject, but the dream and facts of mental pathology sufficiently show that he can also ignore it. However, obsessed by the idea that the essence of psychological life is the fact of being "for oneself," psychologists refuse to recognize this ignorance; they want at any price to save the "for oneself," although this rescue is, in certain cases, equivalent to murder. This is how the hypothesis of the unconscious was born.

But, by denying the unconscious, we only renounce this absurd exigence that asks from the object of a science, to be, at the same time, the builder of this science. And it is because we renounce every device of abstraction that guarantees the reality of the unconscious facts so that we do not have to wonder how we need to conceive its content, after the negation of the unconscious. *This content does not exist.* The subject dreamed: that is all he had to do. He does not know the meaning of the dream; he does not have to know it as pure and simple subject, for this knowledge concerns the psychologist; in short, the latent content, that is, the knowledge of the meaning of the dream, can be *before analysis* neither conscious nor unconscious; it does not exist because science does not result from the scientist's work.

As long as the psychological fact is defined as a simple inner reality, the paradoxical character of the exigence of the omniscience of the subject concerning his inner life cannot break apart, for the science of self being simply relative to a reality, we can not only postulate, but also because of some steps about which we do not have to elaborate here, state the existence of a *sui generis* intuition that immediately grasps the forms of the *sixth essence*. But when it no longer concerns grasping entities or qualities, but rather understanding the meaning of a behavior; when it does not deal with "assisting the unfolding of a life given immediately for oneself," but analyzing the concrete drama of the individual life, then we can no longer ask the subject to be an actor at the same time as being an intelligent spectator only by requiring from him the accomplishment of a work of knowledge which can result only from a proceeding as complex as Freudian analysis.

It is true then to say that conscious and unconscious are together in the same condemnation: the stumbling block of the two theses is established by the fact that they are both founded on the postulate of the "thought for oneself" or of the narrative thought. And that is why the negation of the unconscious does not lead us to the affirmation of the exclusivity of consciousness, and that the negation of this exclusivity does not imply the introduction of the unconscious: the confusion that the postulate in question produces is incompatible with concrete psychology. For the primordial psychological fact is the dramatic life of man, and concrete psychology which seeks to know it only expects this dramatic life from the subject. Classical psychology, on the contrary, asks for more: it asks for a work of knowledge, and also wants to make of this exigence the fundamental statement of psychology. But, *life and knowledge are not synonymous*: the subject who has psychological life does not have to have, at the same time, psychological knowledge; otherwise psychology is useless. The paradox of classical psychology is precisely to eliminate itself as a science from the position of its first principle. How to qualify as science what is only the story of a vision? Concrete psychology, on the contrary, eliminates this paradox, for it does not claim for psychological knowledge any privileged structure, and not asking the subject to be a psychologist, it finds it natural that he is not; and it is precisely because it does not consider that the ignorance of the subject concerning his own psychological being is a particularly remarkable fact that it has no need for the notion of the unconscious.

Our critique of the unconscious arrives at an entirely negative conclusion: the unconscious is only an appearance of which it is possible to demonstrate the falsehood, and Freud's attempt, which consists in wanting to make of the notion of the unconscious a *positive* notion whose affirmation can have a true psychological value, being relative not to simple *absences* or latencies, but to effective *presences*, has completely failed.

We would be wrong, however, in therefore wanting to conclude the uselessness of all that has been done for the unconscious by Freud's predecessors and by Freud himself. For once it is understood that the unconscious does not represent any progress from the *dogmatic* point of view because it is only a way of saving the "for oneself" together with all classical psychology, and that it is not inseparable from psychoanalysis, because it is incompatible with concrete psychology. In short, once it is understood that the theories using the unconscious cannot claim, as they actually do, to represent the truth, the Freudian constructions, and, in general, the whole movement which has oriented psychologists more and more toward the notion of the unconscious, seem to us again singularly interesting.

We have, indeed, seen that the unconscious is modeled after the classical conception of psychological life and with the image of the facts that are given for oneself. But, besides this, whatever the psychological falsehood of the unconscious is, it remains that the facts of the unconscious are no longer immediately given, but are built as the ones of ordinary science. Thus, the fact that psychologists have finally decided to accept this notion reveals to us the weakening and the wearing out of the classical ideal. In other words, the movement toward the unconscious belongs to a decisive moment of the dissolution of classical psychology, to a moment when, while still wanting to save abstraction, psychology started to detach itself from it.

CHAPTER FIVE

The Duality of the Abstract and of the Concrete in Psychoanalysis and the Problem of Concrete Psychology

It is true that psychoanalysis presents an essential duality. It announces concrete psychology by the problems that arise and the way in which it conducts its investigations, but it later denies it by the abstract character of the notions it uses, or that it creates, and the models it uses. And we can say without paradox that Freud is also as amazingly abstract in his theories as he is concrete in his discoveries. This is the result of the preceding analyses.

But as we have already said, it would be too simple to explain this contrast by any lack of clarity or lack of consequence of Freud's thought. Errors of this kind always correspond to historical necessities and go beyond the power of individual logic. But because it is so, there can be no solution of true continuity between the errors and the truth itself: after having condemned, for methodological necessities, the abstract attitude, the critique must show, so that no mystery subsists, that Freud's attitude represents a necessary step in the evolution which arrives at the evidence of the concrete attitude.

But one can say that we make the work seem too easy. We do not seem to notice that the very fact of the duality in question risks compromising our enterprise, at least as we want to present not a concrete psychology that we would have imagined *a priori*, but precisely the one that psychoanalysis gives us. The way in which we interpret the duality in question may not be the only possible one. For this duality can also come from the fact that we interpret psychoanalysis in a way which is exact only to a certain limit, and the duality would then be relative to an interpretation which, not being valid in all psychoanalysis, necessarily divides it into two parts, the second one measuring the inaccuracy of the conception that we have of psychoanalysis. Did not the interpreters of great philosophical doctrines, for example, often admit of dualities of this kind, uniquely because of preconceived ideas and unilateral comprehensions? And is it not true that we had continually to distort Freud's formula to show what we call the concrete inspiration of psychoanalysis? These distortions are possible and can seem legitimate up to a certain limit, but sooner or later the artificial character of such a method necessarily breaks down. And that is when the illusion of duality appears.

It is not enough, in these conditions, to show the historical necessity of what we call Freud's errors. For this demonstration can be only a paraphrase of our illusion. We need to go further: we need to show — and this time without touching Freud's formulas — that in spite of their technical form that is entirely turned toward abstraction, the Freudian speculations also imply an attitude that only needs to be recognized and released in its purity to be the one of concrete psychology.

This demonstration is possible. But its possibility only augments the danger that results from this duality we had to recognize within psychoanalysis. For if, on the one hand, Freud's theoretical speculations only represent an attitude that is already concrete, but disguised in a technical form which is abstract, and if, on the other hand, this disguise is necessary, it is no longer the accuracy of our interpretation that is questioned, but the sufficiency of the conception that we have of concrete psychology. One can tell us, indeed, that concrete psychology, such as we claim to see it at the base of psychoanalysis, is capable of revealing things that have remained inaccessible to classical psychology, which, however, takes its revenge as soon as it deals with theoretical elaboration, so that the so-called return to abstraction can only be the revelation of the *theoretical powerlessness* of our concrete psychology. Thus, there are two possibilities: either we have really guessed the essence of concrete psychology, but then the duality that we have seen shows us that this psychology must resort to the theoretical device of classical psychology which, far from being condemned, receives a new vitality, and since the opposition between the two forms of psychology ceases to be irreducible, our fundamental thesis collapses; or, if we really believe in the death of classical psychology, it is our conception of concrete psychology that loses all interest, for it seems incapable of understanding the drama that it claims to study. Also, if psychoanalysis really announces this concrete psychology that we have defined, it seems devoid of interest, in the light of our interpretation, since it presents itself as one more aborted attempt. In short, whichever way we go, this duality of which the statement could appear at first as a victory of our method is, in reality, a defeat.

It is obvious that these arguments are valid only if the duality in question is truly absolute; that is, if we are not able to show concrete psychology as we have defined it truly at work not only when it deals with the definition of the fact and of the conception of the method, but with the very understanding of the human drama. But it must collapse if we can show that, far from suffering a theoretical powerlessness, it has already started to expand its fundamental notions.

I

The contrast between the concrete conception of the fact and of the method, on the one hand, and the abstractness of the explanations, on the other, is explained with Freud first by the way he conceives the connections between psychology and psychoanalysis. Freud starts from this idea that psychoanalysis is a particular proceeding which, while allowing one to find new results to which the methods of classical psychology would never have led, does not end up at the "psychology" of the facts in question. His fundamental idea is that psychoanalysis and psychology are on two different levels: the psychoanalytic attitude is something other than the search for a psychology of facts, while the search for the psychological explanation implies the abandonment of the properly psychoanalytic attitude.

This attitude is very well expressed in the *Traumdeutung*: after having described the facts that psychoanalysis allows one to discover, Freud searches their explanation in a different section, more precisely, in the section entitled "Psychology of the Dream Processes." Until now, it concerned interpreting and analyzing the dream; now it is about *explaining* it:

> We dealt, until now, essentially with discovering the hidden meaning of dreams, what path helps in finding it again, and what are the means that the work of the dream used to conceal it. It was the exigencies of the interpretation of dreams which were, until now, at the center of our interest. (4th ed., Germ., 404)

We must now enter "a new path": to understand the dream as a psychological phenomenon.

To explain a psychological fact means for Freud to bring it back to *known laws of psychology*. About regression he tells us: "We did not, as we might think, explain this character of the dream, we did not bring it back to known laws of psychology" (541). Consequently, the theoretical part of Freud's enterprise is immediately announced as an attempt to bring back the psychoanalytic facts to classical psychology, and what appeared to us as an absolutely radical change of orientation is seen with Freud in the most natural way: by the simple fact that we are looking for the explanation, we find ourselves brought back to classical psychology.

In these circumstances, the originality of psychoanalysis will be translatable on the level of explanation only by the fact that there is, in classical psychology, nothing that is ready to receive the new facts discovered by Freud. "It is impossible," he says, "to explain the dream as a psychological phenomenon, for to explain means returning to what is already known; but, there has existed until now no psychological notion to which we could connect the elements with which our analysis ends" (508). Only, this insufficiency is not *constitutive*, it does not reveal a primordial and definitive powerlessness, but simply a *temporary imperfection* that we will be able to remedy. But whatever the extent and the newness of the work of broadening that is imposed here, the latter will leave the very foundations of classical psychology intact. All that results then, from the newness of psychoanalytic discoveries is the obligation of "making new hypotheses about the structure of the psychic apparatus and the actions of its forces."

It is enough, then, to glimpse at the "implications" that Freud develops and the hypotheses he makes, to see that, for him, it exclusively concerns building a structure consistent with the scientific ideal of psychologists at the end of the nineteenth century.

We know the scientific ideal very well: physiological, energetic and quantitative dreaming make up its main traits. What we are looking for is a psychic mechanism that reminds one of the schemes that physics uses in its explanations, that following the energistic movement in physics, psychologists have also abandoned mechanical models to shift toward energic schemes. Freud sometimes expresses this classical ideal in the most naive way: "Libido," he says in *Group Psychology and Analysis of the Ego* (trans. French, 1924, p. 36) "is a term borrowed from the theory of emotionalism. We so name energy, considered as a quantitative magnitude (not yet measurable) of the tendencies connected to what we call love." And the developments of chapter 3 sufficiently show Freud's ingenuity as he tries to fulfill the ideal in question.

It is clear that Freud himself has never doubted the central edifice of classical psychology. Its methods can be imperfect, classical psychologists could be prejudiced and stubborn on certain questions, but all this changes only the *theses* and not the *foundations*: classical psychology must be worked on, but it requires only a work of revision and elaboration.

Once we have adopted this attitude, it is impossible to stop, and never will the incompatibility of the new facts with traditional psychology break apart, for it will always be possible to push further and further the content and the expansion of its hypotheses and notions. That is why Freud can only do the speculative work such as he announced it, without ever realizing that he goes backward in the path of his own discoveries. And if by doing this purely formal work, which is only the mechanical unfolding of various models, we can really think that we have *explained*, it is thanks to the fact that we are precisely "attached" to the scientific ideal of classical psychology.

Considered in its theoretical phase, Freud's enterprise represents the antipode of ours. We wanted to develop the psychology that is contained in psychoanalytic facts and method, whereas, for Freud, it is the reverse problem: which is the form of classical psychology from which psychoanalytic facts can be deduced and, as this does not exist, needs to be invented.

It is obvious, at first sight, that Freud's attitude is the first that appears and does so in a most natural way. We discover, with the help of psychoanalysis, a certain number of facts: they are *immediately* considered as facts of inner life. This idea is so natural that there are some texts where Freud considers free association as a form of reflection or introspection. It is understood, in these conditions, that all psychoanalysis brings us is information on this inner reality that classical psychology wants to study: all progress in the psychoanalytic discoveries then becomes necessarily a motive to go further in the development of our ideas on "the psychic apparatus."

Considering this "fixation" to the ideal of classical psychology that is general in his era, Freud is led to take the attitude that we just described. The only thing that could have stopped him would have been precisely to separate himself from this ideal. But that was impossible, considering that by his very position he gives classical psychology a purely formal problem that not only the latter, but also any theoretical group, true or false, can easily resolve.

Freud gets to psychology by starting from psychoanalysis. At that moment, his discoveries are already made and his attitude is no longer *creative*, but purely disinterested: he does not expect from psychology the accomplishment of a fruitful and productive work, but only the insertion in a network of notions and hypotheses of discoveries already made. And so Freud cannot notice the fundamental sterility of psychology, because it gives it a problem whose solution implies only an *expansion*.

Freud's attitude was therefore inevitable for two reasons. First because, considering the fundamental ideas of the era, psychoanalytic discoveries immediately appear as psychological facts in the classical sense of the word, and later because, approaching psychology once the truly creative work is already finished, the powerlessness of psychology cannot burst forth. In other words, a pure psychoanalyst whose essential occupation is the very practice of the psychoanalytic method, necessarily had to arrive at this contradiction that we have shown in Freud's work.

It is different for someone who goes, not from psychoanalysis to psychology, but from psychology to psychoanalysis. For when the emphasis is on psychology itself, we do not approach it once the work of creation is finished, to be satisfied with this deceitful operation that consists of extending hypotheses as an afterthought in order to explain some facts discovered without their intervention, but it is from psychology itself that we expect power and productivity. The history of psychology and its actual occupations are here to show that never would the classical conception of the fact and of the method have allowed one to pose problems in this way, which has led psychoanalysts to discoveries precisely where the classical methods had failed.

It is obvious, in these conditions, that the discoveries of psychoanalysis presuppose a conception of psychology that cannot coincide with classical psychology and that they pose a new problem, the problem that consists in knowing, not with the help of those complementary speculations of which we can reduce the new facts to the old models, but which consists of this new psychology that made the discoveries possible.

Such is the attitude that we have adopted in the present work. However, this attitude presupposes Freud's attitude and could only have come after it. For, first of all, psychoanalysts are the ones who made these discoveries whose analysis ends up with concrete psychology, and they had to start by trying to find an explanation. Thus, the latter could not avoid ending up, for the reasons we just discussed, with the duality between the fundamental inspiration and the theoretical device.

But this duality was necessary for an enterprise like ours to be born. By seeing the wealth of psychoanalytic discoveries and of the poverty of classical psychology, the abstract speculations of psychoanalysis present a paradox that imperiously calls for a critique.

II

Considering the way in which Freud poses the problem of the explanation, the originality of psychoanalysis can be revealed, as we said earlier, only by the necessity of expanding the notions of classical psychology, and of introducing into it new hypotheses that remain, however, consistent with its fundamental procedures.

Because the notional works need to be molded on the new facts brought by psychoanalysis, it would be amazing that in spite of their abstract behavior, they would not keep something of this concrete inspiration which gave life to the discoveries.

The unconscious has appeared to us until now as the height of abstraction. This is perfectly true: it owes its origins to these procedures we call abstract; they produce it and without them it cannot have any sense. Thus, there is at the bottom of all theory and more deeply situated than the steps that give it its technical form, a general attitude that allows the theory in question to go beyond its own dogmatic signification. Such is the case of the hypothesis of the unconscious: whatever the incompatibility of its technical aspect with concrete psychology may be, its acceptance implies an attitude that is completely contrary to the ideal of classical psychology.

What essentially characterizes the unconscious in general and independently from the Freudian theory is that it relates to psychological facts whose subject has no direct knowledge, or which are not given to him in an immediate intuition. Consequently, the introduction of the unconscious will mean the end of the hegemony of introspection, since unconscious facts, while being psychological, escape consciousness and introspection, whatever it is, and we thus admit a group of psychological facts that are not given "for oneself," and for the stating and the study of which we need to resort to other methods.

What is remarkable in this consequence of the introduction of the unconscious is not the fact that we are forced to renounce introspection. Classical psychologists do not find this difficult to do and they often abandon introspection for "objective" methods, physiological, biological, or other. But we need to notice that in these cases, and from admission of the psychologists of whom we speak, it concerns abandoning the area of the psychic. For, when we abandon introspection for any of the "objective" methods, it is always in accordance with a definition or a hypothesis that allows one to give a place in psychology — even the whole area — to the physiological excitations and reactions, or to the purely motive aspect of behaviors. And thus we do not abandon introspection to study the *psychological facts themselves* by objective methods, but only objective facts that we could relate to the first ones. And it is all the more true that whenever we talk about the "psychic," we are forced to return to introspection whether we like it or not, and under one pretext or another.

The hypothesis of the unconscious, on the contrary, means that *introspection has become insufficient for the exploration of the psychic.*

In fact, for all those who recognized the psychological unconscious, this signifies a group of facts that are as really and as currently psychological as the conscious facts, "with one exception," as Freud says, "they lack consciousness." It therefore does not mean renouncing introspection because we want to give objective facts a psychological signification, but because it is the psychic itself that goes beyond the *for itself* ("pour soi").

This is precisely how, in a sense, the unconscious announces concrete psychology. First, a psychology that uses the notion of the unconscious will need to renounce the integral affirmation of the privileged nature of psychological knowledge. We will no longer be able to assert that it is unique in its kind because it immediately grasps its object, considering that it is precisely in this "grasping" that the proper being of the psychological fact resides, for there exist some facts that, while being psychological, are outside the *for itself*. They can thus be known only in a *mediate* way, either because of the intervention of an external observer, or because of proceedings of reasoning similar to ones the other sciences use.

In other words, even though the unconscious appears, in one sense, more mysterious than consciousness, in another sense it represents, the first step in the destruction of psychological mystery. For certain psychic phenomena, at least, the subject of knowledge is not in a more privileged situation than when it faces any object. In this way, psychologists who subscribe to the notion of the unconscious lose the habit of considering all psychological facts as the simple themes of a *sui generis* perception, considering that the unconscious facts must be built, or at least rebuilt.

We end up within classical psychology at a duality that consists of a very powerful dialectical ferment. After the introduction of the unconscious, we can no longer define psychological fact by the *for itself*: the classical definition of psychological fact is questioned precisely on the very *level of the psychic*. We then find ourselves faced with two kinds of "the psychical": one whose knowledge is a *perception*, but also another one that is only a *construction* — one that we continue to define by the *for itself*; the other, which is impossible to define in this way. Thus, it is evident that the psychological facts, whether they are conscious or unconscious, participate in the same essence, and this essence is situated deeper than consciousness since the conscious facts can become unconscious, without losing their psychological essence. By pursuing research in this direction, we find ourselves led to defining psychological facts independently of the *for itself*; that is, independently of a *sui generis* perception, and the problem that is then posed is the very problem of concrete psychology: *to define the psychic as it is*; that is, by avoiding all confusion with physiology, biology or any other science of nature or of man as being nature, while *abstracting the hypothesis according to which the psychic is given in a sui generis perception*. In other words, simultaneously to admit a psychical phenomenon that is given and another which is constructed is impossible, and the idea that there exists a *constructed psychical phenomenon* invites generalization, and we are then led to seek the originality of the psychical phenomenon somewhere else than in this originality, so to speak, chemical, that is at the foundation of the classical definition. In short, the fundamental attitude that is at the base of the hypothesis of the unconscious already contains the negation of psychological realism, and the consequent development of this hypothesis would have led to the search for a definition of psychological fact that excludes realism.

Only, classical psychology has never reached either the recognition of the true meaning of the hypothesis of the unconscious nor the systematic development of its consequences, and after having shown the duality in question, it purely and simply maintained it. Owing to the fundamentally abstract character of classical psychology, realism was capable of intervening in order to stop the movement that would clearly have ended up with its destruction.

After placing the unconscious next to the conscious, we got around the difficulty by making consciousness a *quality* that could be added or not to the *psychic*, and then the duality is resolved by defining the psychological fact consistently with realism, simply by the psychological being *pure*, but whose originality remains, of course, *chemical*.

Freud is led, for reasons we have shown elsewhere,[1] to give to the unconscious a role and a much more important place than classical psychologists had done. Consequently, we will find with Freud, on the one hand, a more rigorous development of the purely technical implications of the hypothesis, and, on the other hand, an even larger approximation of concrete psychology, in the very sense that we indicated earlier.

The Freudian theory gives, from the technical point of view, two affirmations:

1. Consciousness is only a superior [i.e., outer] organ of perception;
2. The unconscious is transcendental relative to consciousness.

At least one part of the first affirmation is already implied in the notion of the unconscious. Indeed, the very fact of introducing the unconscious implies the extension of the definition of the psychological fact, and this one will be defined, according to realism, as *the psychic in general*[2] whose existence does not necessarily require consciousness. The acquisition of the conscious character for the psychic can then be easily assimilated to a perception, and precisely because the very *being* of the psychic is independent of consciousness, the model of the perception is applicable here. Meanwhile, the affirmation that consciousness is solely an organ of perception already implies psychoanalysis. For, in classical psychology the unconscious does not play a sufficiently important role to prevent us from asserting that, beside the facts for which consciousness is only an organ of perception, there are others of which it constitutes the being itself. But Freud's attitude must be much more radical. Psychoanalysis, indeed, had to include in the unconscious all the important and truly determining processes so that while the dream, for example, could be explained in detail by preconscious or unconscious activities, there remained for consciousness only the pure and simple perception of the psychic.

The second affirmation is based on psychoanalytic considerations. The result, indeed, of Freud's analyses is that the psychic is admitted to the perception of consciousness only under certain conditions. Consequently, the perception of the psychic being necessarily relative to these conditions, the unconscious in itself is an *unknown*.[3]

These two fundamental affirmations of the Freudian theory of the unconscious only stress the progress of abstract psychology towards concrete psychology, and this attitude that we have found behind the hypothesis of the unconscious is thus rendered quite conspicuous.

It is no longer a question of saying that besides the conscious phenomena we need also to consider the unconscious phenomena. On the contrary, the result of Freud's analyses is that consciousness cannot teach us anything about what really interests us, for what is important to know for the explanation belongs either to the preconscious or to the unconscious. And far from being capable of stopping at consciousness, the psychoanalyst must begin by going beyond it: if we want to understand the dream, we must abandon the manifest content and proceed toward the latent content. We can no longer say, in these conditions, that the introduction of the unconscious breaks up the hegemony of introspection on a particular point. Considering the role of the unconscious in psychoanalysis, introspection is no longer a scientific method in the proper sense of the word, for what can be known by introspection is not yet a psychological knowledge: the psychoanalyst does not stop at the *introspection* of the manifest content. Thus the psychologist no longer finds himself faced with two categories of facts, some immediately known and others mediately known, for all the facts that are truly effective are found in the unconscious. In that way the psychologist will only deal with mediate knowledge: the mystery of psychological knowledge has entirely disappeared and the psychoanalyst will have to create a method that, while being neither physiological nor biological, and that, in a word, while being exclusively *psychological*, is, however, something quite other than introspection. This method is the psychoanalytic technique that is precisely the "royal path that leads to the knowledge of the unconscious."

Thus, there has been a Copernican revolution: all the interest of psychologists went from the themes of the immediate psychological perception toward the themes that can no longer be considered as such, but which are *constructed*, and in this very way the whole ideology of classical psychology finds itself challenged.

Only once more, or rather, one last time, realism intervenes to prevent its own destruction. We will continue to interpret the mediate themes with which psychologists deal as relating to a reality and by choosing the last possibility that remains to save realism; we assert that the reality in question is *transcendental* and that we grasp it only in its "phenomena." And indeed, Freud explains the dream and psychoneuroses, and everything in general by "noumenal" activities.

But such an attitude can have no stability. For the affirmation that a certain reality is known only in its phenomena always endangers the reality in question, and we will, sooner or later, have to limit knowledge solely to phenomena. Only, this "phenomenism" must be other than the one spoken of by psychologists of the "psychology without a soul," since the reality that we go back to is not simply the soul as substance, but the psychic as a reality, in short, *the inner life*.

Freud himself remains dogmatic. With the help of the realistic approach, he goes beyond phenomena. But he does it so ostensibly, and the approach is articulated with such clearness, that his dogmatism prepares the corresponding critique and announces a "critical" psychology that will deserve this name, not because it will be a psychology without a soul, but because it will be a psychology without inner life, and in spite of it, without the least trace of physiology or even biology.

We can therefore show that the duality between the abstract and the concrete within psychoanalysis is not simply an optical illusion, but that it translates the particular nature of the Freudian attitude. For not only was the return to the abstract necessarily supposed to occur in psychoanalysis, but also the resulting theories such as they are, and in spite of their abstract technical form imply, the very attitude that is at the root of concrete psychology. In short, it is not with us, but with Freud himself, that we notice an *optical illusion*.

If Freud's position is, in this way, determined with sufficient precision, which it does not seem to be, it is concrete psychology itself. For all we know positively until now is the way in which the psychological fact is defined as being a segment of this "drama" that constitutes the life of the particular individual and the method that it claims to use to study it. But we have not yet seen the way in which it fulfills its promises; in other words, we have not yet seen concrete psychology at work in the analysis of the drama, with notions appropriate to its level and to its inspiration. And for the abstract character of the Freudian speculations not to be considered as the revelation of the theoretical powerlessness of concrete psychology as we conceive it, we must show that among all the notions and hypotheses that Freud was led to build, there are some that, while being on the same level as others, already belong to concrete psychology.

III

To show concrete psychology at work, we must show the true character of a certain number of new notions that Freud was led to introduce following the analysis of dreams and neuroses, and which play a dominant role in the technical explanations. We basically, are considering two of them: identification and the Oedipus complex.[4]

Identification consists of the fact that "the ego absorbs, so to speak, the properties of the object" (*Group Psychology and Analysis of the Ego*, trans. French, 60). A child "having had the misfortune of losing a kitten suddenly said that he was this kitten, started to crawl, did not want to eat at the table anymore, etc." (63).

We should not confuse the Freudian *identification* with the *imitation* of classical psychology, "the immediate transition from a perception, mostly visual, to a movement reproducing the cause of perception." Even though we can discuss our definition to replace *static* terms by *dynamic* terms, what is clear is that such a definition that abstracts the very *sense* of the act in question, is entirely formal: we only stop at the general mechanism of the act. The fact that this mechanism is described in terms of elements or in terms of attitudes does not change anything of its formal character. Furthermore, the subject is eliminated not only because in most cases we will make of the imitation a small drama in the third person whose actors are the *elements*, but also because, considering formalism, it is not a question of considering imitation as being in its content something of the life of the particular individual. Far from having us face this life, on the contrary, imitation moves us further away: it appears as a general function such as habit, for example, or memory, and all that classical psychology is able to do is to look for its general mechanism, to describe its general development, in short, to study it *in itself*.

Identification is, on the contrary, essentially an act that has a meaning: for the subject, it concerns *being* someone else or something else than himself, it is about conforming to a model by adopting so to speak all its dialectics. "The genesis of masculine homosexuality (62)," says Freud,

> is, most often, the following: the young man has remained for a long time and intensely, fixated to his mother, in the sense of the *Oedipus complex*. Once puberty has been reached, the young man must exchange his mother for another sexual object. A sudden change of direction occurs: instead of letting go of his mother, he identifies with her, becomes her and looks for objects susceptible to replace his own "ego" and that he can love and take care of as he was loved

and taken care of by his mother. This is a process of which we can observe the reality as often as we like and that is, naturally, completely independent of any hypothesis that we could formulate about the reasons and the motives of this sudden transformation. What is striking in this identification, is its intensity; in a more important context, especially from the point of view of the character, the individual undergoes a transformation according to the model of the person who had served until now as a libidinal object.

In these conditions, far from being eliminated, the subject is integrally implied in the identification that becomes, not only an effective part of his life, but also the key to a whole series of attitudes that are only understood through it. In that way, too, the identification always brings us back to the life of the particular individual, for it is this alone that will enable us to reconstitute its *signification*. Identification is therefore a concrete notion: it is etched within the human drama itself; in other words, it is a segment of the life of the particular individual.

The Oedipus complex is well known, and we only need a simple allusion to it. The young boy has for his mother an emotional attachment of an erotic nature, in the broadest sense that this term has for psychoanalysts. Later, "the little one notices that the father prevents access to his mother; his identification with the father takes hostile tint and ends up being confused with the desire to replace the father by the mother" (58).

Certainly the term *complex* reveals the psychology of the *Vorstellung*, since the *complex* is for Freud a representation charged with a great emotional intensity. But — and it will be useless to demonstrate it this time[5] — this is only a question of style. In fact, the Oedipus complex is not a *process*, and even less a *state*, but is a *dramatic model*, or, if we prefer, a *human behavior*.

In the notion of identification and in the Oedipus complex, there are two notions that satisfy the essential condition that the notions of concrete psychology must fulfill: they remain on the level of the "I," and are etched in the very matter of the human drama. There no longer remains in them any trace of the realism of classical psychology. Neither identification nor the Oedipus complex represent the themes of an original perception and they are not related to a reality of some chemical kind.

The reality to which they are related, indeed, is only the reality of the human drama, that of the *signification* that constitutes a *human scene* of a *group of movements*.

Neither identification, nor the Oedipus complex is based on the consideration of a group of inner states or psychophysiological mechanisms; they are not even *mental attitudes*, since they represent integral procedures and express the human form of a scene, and nothing else. These notions have some value only on the level of the dramatic actions of man, and they are incompatible with the realism of the *sixth essence*.

Identification and the Oedipus complex are complexes only from the point of view of the act that constitutes them. And being explicative notions, they are, on the contrary, primitive.

Introspective psychology would describe the inner states that duplicate the identification; representations, feelings, or, if we prefer, mental attitudes and qualities that the fact of living the form of another implies. We would then arrive at the touching analyses of sympathy.

Experimental psychology would attack the positive side of the identification. We would study the sensori-motor and ideo-motor mechanisms to elaborate physiological myths. We would then arrive at imitation.

But, in any case, the explanation would go beyond the identification to try to reconstitute it with the help of elements that are above or below it; that is, with the help of elements that are either psychological, or physiological. For Freud, on the contrary, identification and the Oedipus complex are elementary notions that must precisely help the analysis and the reconstitution of the human drama.

Identification and the Oedipus complex are not only the segments of the life of a particular individual, but are also great dramatic models having, so to speak, their own dialectics, which can, consequently, provide the key to a whole series of attitudes.

It is not even necessary to consider the analysis of dreams and of psychoneuroses: the mere observation of daily life shows the great importance of the attitudes expressed by these notions. It is enough to look around to see that our whole human life is crossed by them and that they direct us most often in the actions that will have a determining influence on our whole destiny.

From the technical point of view, identification has explained above the genesis of homosexuality in man. It also intervenes in the Freudian theory of hysteria,[6] of love,[7] in the explanation that he attempted in hypnosis,[8] of character,[9] etc. As far as the Oedipus complex is concerned, we know what an important role Freud gave it in his explanations.

What is remarkable is that identification and the Oedipus complex are explanatory concepts. For Freud satisfies this other exigence of concrete psychology, according to which the most elementary notions must still be acts, acts of the "I" and of the segments of dramatic life.[10] For, instead of considering them as the starting point of an analysis in the sense of classical psychology, he makes of them elementary notions that will help reconstitute behaviors as complex as love, for example. But, identification and the Oedipus complex are precisely the acts of the "I" and of the segments of the life of the particular individual. And also, concrete psychology can analyze the drama, while not transforming it into impersonal drama: the *elements* that it uses are models in the first person.

It is true that the notions that we have just considered are not conceived by Freud consistently with their true essence. They are placed on the same level as others of an abstract origin. Furthermore, the elementary analysis, in the sense of classical psychology, is not entirely absent: the expression *Oedipus complex*, on the one hand, and the Freudian definition of the term *complex* on the other, sufficiently prove it. And although Freud was led, in his last works, as for example, *Group Psychology and Analysis of the Ego*, and *The Ego and the Id*, to base his explanations more and more on his notions without dwelling too long on elementary analysis, the latter is far from being absent, and duality still persists.

Only, this duality is, as it were, much more evolved than the one that we stated, by analyzing the theory of the unconscious. The fundamental attitude that already reveals the inspiration of concrete psychology is still entirely covered by the technical form that is produced by the abstract. Here, on the contrary, it concerns notions that are concrete in their own technical form and on which is grafted the abstract attitude, in spite of the fact that they are used elsewhere in a way that suits them. These notions no longer have a hold on the latter, and even though they are indistinctly mixed in the statement itself, the abstract attitude, on one hand, and the concrete attitude, on the other, are formed separately. For we can easily notice that the elementary analysis applied to notions like identification and the Oedipus complex is detached from these notions and that they, and the way in which they allow us the analysis of the drama, are the ones that alone, retain our attention.

Whether these notions are definitive or not, that they are as important as Freud thinks, has no importance from the point of view of the very vitality of concrete psychology. The main thing is that they can show us that concrete psychology is not only capable of formulating exigencies that it cannot meet and of conceiving a method that it is egregiously incapable of applying, but that it is qualified to analyze, and it does so consistently with its own exigencies, the human drama of which it makes the supreme domain of psychology.

These notions and the way Freud uses them in his explanations show us that a psychology that only deals with the human drama, that incorporates, in his explanations, only notions that, though they are *elementary*, already represent human acts, only, in short, *a psychology that never leaves this level, neither in searching for facts, nor in their theoretical elaboration*, is perfectly viable, since it is already alive. The question of principle being thus resolved, everything else is only a technical question.

The Virtues of Concrete Psychology and the Problems it Presents

1. We have studied psychoanalysis in the *Traumdeutung* to derive from this study a lesson for psychology. We found in Freud a new inspiration contrary to that of classical psychology, and we have then shown that the true opposition between psychoanalysis and official psychology is that of two irreducible forms of psychology: abstract psychology and concrete psychology. It is by delving into the way in which Freud poses the problems and conceives his method that we managed to reveal the main characteristics of concrete psychology, and once we were in possession of these exigencies, they allowed us to discover the fundamental procedures of classical psychology, such as *realism, formalism*, and *abstraction*.

2. The information that we could obtain, with the help of psychoanalysis, about the exigencies of concrete psychology, was revealed as an efficient instrument of critique in the analysis of abstract psychology. It happens, however, that this concrete psychology, issued from psychoanalysis, must begin by turning against the latter and to serve as principle to an inner critique: indeed, we had to verify with Freud, especially at the time of the theoretical elaboration of the facts, a frank return to abstraction. This return is very clear and we have established its existence, not only through our remarks made on notions that Freud introduced in the *Traumdeutung*, but especially by showing that classical procedures alone permit one

151

to give a meaning to the hypothesis of the unconscious. We have thus rediscovered within psychoanalysis itself the opposition between concrete psychology and abstract psychology.

3. To ensure that the verification of this duality does not turn itself against our enterprise, we have shown not only that the "Freudian errors" represent a necessary step in the development of concrete psychology, but also that concrete psychology as it results from psychoanalysis can do much more than conceive a scientific ideal and formulate exigencies, considering that it is already alive at the present time, because in psychoanalysis itself there exist a certain number of notions and explanations which, being integrally consistent with the exigencies of concrete psychology, prove its vitality by this very fact.

4. Along the way, we have expressed this opinion according to which concrete psychology such as we conceive it is precisely that which is called to fulfill the dream, already old, of a positive psychology, for it alone has accomplished this radical reform of the understanding that the truly scientific attitude implies and which classical psychologists want to economize by substituting for it a purely surface imitation of scientific methods.

This "reform of the understanding" we are talking about essentially consists of the fact that by formulating the exigencies of scientific psychology, we need to go to the end, with no reservations and no pity. For it is not enough to formulate exigencies. Exigencies to which no reality corresponds represent nothing, and it is only later, once they are realized, that those who had formulated them will acquire the value of having dreamed the truth. Classical psychologists often confuse exigencies and their realization. Thus, in fact, their psychology could never fulfill the exigencies of a positive psychology such as they were formulated at the birth of modern psychology. That is why positive psychology exists in today's official psychology only as a dream.

5. It will suffice, to demonstrate this point, to talk about those of our preceding developments that helped us establish that the procedures of classical psychology cannot have any *psychological* meaning. For, indeed, how could we qualify as psychological science a theoretical group to which there corresponds no psychological reality? This demonstration will be excellent when we realize the truth about concrete psychology. But for now, as we are far from

it, we can reproach it for being purely formal: since by psychology we understand the opposite of classical psychology, it is natural that the procedures of the latter can have no *psychological* sense. That is why we must show, here, something else: we need to show that concrete psychology is the first positive psychology, because it has succeeded in resolving the problems posed but never resolved by classical psychology in spite of the number and divergence of attempts: *to satisfy the conditions of existence of a positive psychology.*

6. These are the three conditions of existence:

a. Psychology must be *a posteriori* a science, that is, the adequate study of a group of facts;
b. It must be original; that is, it must study facts that are irreducible to the objects of other sciences;
c. It must be objective; it must, in other words, define the psychological fact and method in such a way that they are, rightfully and universally accessible and verifiable.

Thus, it is enough to look at the history of psychology in the last 50 years and remember the critiques that helped the destruction of antagonistic tendencies, to immediately see that there has never been, until now, a psychological program capable of satisfying these three conditions at the same time. Far from that, we have generally tried to resolve the problem by sacrificing either condition #2, or condition #3. The precise demonstration of this point would simply be a game of erudition. We know that introspectionist psychologists sacrificed condition #3, and objectivists, condition #2; that is, that to the extent to which the first ones succeeded in saving the purely psychological character of the object of psychology, they took from it all scientific reality, and the others succeeded in putting real facts in the foundation of psychology only by sacrificing the *property* of psychology.

We therefore end up with psychologies which, possessing, so to speak, only half of their essence, are incapable of satisfying the first condition: they cannot be *a posteriori*, for they have to replace, as the followers of physiological psychology do, with *myths* this *science* they dream of, but that they cannot realize. This way too, the psychologies in question are revealed as insufficient, but since the impossibility of satisfying both conditions in question at the same time still persists, we try to resolve the problem by creating either introspections, or unedited objectivities. That is why psychology shows this hopeless oscillation between introspection and the objectivity that has been characterizing its history or 50 years.

7. If we now look for the explanation of this fundamental powerlessness, we rediscover the influence of psychological realism. For classic introspectionist psychology coming directly from realism, the psychological fact is a *simple theme, relating to a perceptible reality* that we call *psychic*. The *property* of psychological facts is therefore given by the participation in this reality that constitutes a world or a life in the same sense as nature, but which enjoys opposed properties. Objectivist psychologists protesting against psychological realism tried to free themselves only from the technical form of realism, but not from the fundamental attitude that produces it: they tried to define the psychological fact as a simple theme relating to a perceptible reality, and even accepting the classical alternative of mind and matter, they found themselves facing an exigence of *looking for the psychological fact in the themes of outer perception.*

8. We need to add that psychologists, who had been the first to advocate objective psychology, did not even succeed in eliminating the technical form of realism. They believed that it would be enough to establish any relation of correspondence between psychological facts, on one hand, and external facts, on the other, so that the problem of objectivity can be resolved. They did not realize that an attempt of this kind could only be a great *ignoratio elenchi* and a *petition of principle — ignoratio elenchi* because it does not concern knowing what the objective aspect of the facts of classical psychology is, but what result that the objective study of the psychic can give; and *petition of principle* because before trying to study the objective aspect of the psychological facts in the classic sense of the word, it is necessary to know if the objective study of the psychological facts will not end up at a totally different result. By trying to study the psychological facts "from the outside," the psychologists in question have accepted *as is* the themes of classical psychology, whereas the new psychology was to question them.

In fact, there has only been one sincere attempt by objective psychology: behaviorism, such as it results from Watson's fundamental ideas. It took 50 years and the successive failures of Wundt, Bechterev and others, and the revelation of the mythological character of physiological psychology as soon as it goes beyond the physiology of sensations, in order that, from the study of animal behavior, there spurt forth at last a positive conception in the rigorous sense of the term.

Watson's great merit, and we said it from the very beginning, is to have finally understood that the ideal of psychology, science of nature, implied a renouncing, absolute and without conditions, of inner life. Until now, objective psychologies were objective only in the forewords of texts and they had the habit of reintroducing introspective notions in the text, with more or less naivete. Watson understood that the sincerely scientific attitude required that we get rid of all that is introspection and spirituality, and he succeeded in what escaped the greatest champions of objective psychology: *think through to the very end the exigence of objectivity in psychology.* By the same token, behaviorism brings a revelation of definitive value, namely that his predecessors in objective psychology, the Wundts, the Bechtherevs and the others are comparable to peripateticians who wanted to weigh the diaphanous and study with the stroboscope the transition from the power to the act.

But even though it succeeds in presenting a conception of psychology consistent with the ideal of objectivity, Watson's attempt is afflicted by the same insufficiency as the preceding ones: it saves objectivity, but loses psychology. The proof is that hardly had Watson begun to draw the conclusions of his discovery that, right away, American psychologists started to look for a *nonphysiological behaviorism.*

Only behavior and its mechanism observed from the outside can interest a behaviorist in the real sense of the word. But then, psychology is so objective that it drowns, so to speak, in objectivity, and all that behaviorism could teach us would be at the level of animal mechanics. This is a desperate solution; behaviorism suppresses the enigma of man and can only replace it with *promises* because it eliminated the property of the psychological fact.

This is one source of the powerlessness of behaviorism as psychology, and the problem of nonphysiological behaviorism.

9. Here again the powerlessness is due to the fact that, in the very position of the problem, it is the motive attitude of classical realism that has acted. Understanding this time with precision that inner life was incompatible with objectivity, Watson simply turned toward outer perception. Certainly, as we will see later, his objective theme is less simplistic than that of his predecessors, but it remains that he has accepted the alternative "inside or outside," the difference

residing in the fact that the outside happens to be, this time, more biological than physiological.

10. The reason psychology cannot be established as a positive science is that, capable of only partially satisfying its conditions of existence, it is locked in the antithesis of objectivity and subjectivity. To escape, we need something other than this vulgar eclecticism which today characterizes the average psychologist; we need a *synthesis* in the proper sense of the term. And if classical psychology is incapable of establishing this synthesis, it is because it believes that the psychological fact must be a perceptive theme. We can then only choose between the classical alternative of inner perception or of outer perception, or resort to both at the same time, which evidently implies the ignorance of the subject.

To overcome the classical antithesis, we would have had to renounce seeing the psychological fact in any perception whatever and consent to placing at the base of psychological science an *act of knowledge of a structure placed higher than the simple perception.* It was the only way of satisfying both conditions of originality and of objectivity; that is, to find an original and objective area, without this originality being that of a new "matter" and without this objectivity being that of physical matter; in short, to escape the alternatives of *inside* and *outside.*

11. Concrete psychology, having abandoned realism with the fundamental attitude it implies, found in the *human drama* a group of facts that satisfy the conditions that we have just stated; it shows itself then as a *true synthesis of subjective psychology and of objective psychology.*

By choosing as a field of study the *drama*, it is not just any perception that is the constitutive act of psychological science. It is not *outer* perception, because its themes are not psychological facts yet, and it is not *inner* perception, because its themes are no longer psychological facts.

A gesture that I make is a psychological fact, because it is a segment of the drama that my life represents. The way it inserts in this drama is given to the psychologist by the story that I can tell about this gesture. But it is the *gesture made clear by the story* that is the psychological fact and not the gesture alone, nor the realized content of the story. The gesture has, indeed, a physiological mechanism, but this mechanism still has nothing human about it;

it cannot then interest the psychologist, as it is not yet psychological. Besides, the content of the story that I can tell about my gesture implies, seen through classical psychology, static or dynamic descriptions, but these descriptions do not interest me either. They imply the abandonment of the meaning for the benefit of formalism and other procedures that we have described, and if the consideration of the purely physiological mechanism of my gesture is on this side of the psychological point of view, the introspective descriptions are beyond: *the psychologist's point of view is the one that coincides with the drama.*

12. In a general way, outer perception can only give us the purely material frame of the drama, and still we need, for it to be so, to have the outer theme defined in Watson's way, namely, by the behavior. But, the psychological fact is not the *simple behavior*, but the *human behavior*; that is, the behavior such as it relates, on the one hand, to events among which human life unfolds, and, on the other, to the individual, inasmuch as he is the subject of this life. In short, the psychological fact is the behavior that has a *human meaning*. Only, to establish this meaning, we need themes that are furnished by the subject and that reach us through the story: the simple motor behavior becomes psychological fact only after being clarified by the story.

In this way that the statement of human behavior results, for the psychologist, not from a simple perception, but from the complicated perception of a *comprehension*. Consequently, the psychological fact is not a *simple* theme: as object of knowledge, it is essentially *constructed*.

13. We cannot say, besides, that the "meaning of the drama" is given only by the *inner experience* the subject has of his behaviors, and that, consequently, if we can go beyond the simple outer perception of motor behavior to reach human behavior, it is because, so to speak, on the other side, *the inner aspect of behavior is revealed.* It is obvious that we are referring to the story that the individual can give us about his behavior. The story in question, then, is essentially a *significative* story, and psychology deals with it only to the extent to which it makes the drama clear. To see in the story something other than the materials destined to make the drama clear would mean accomplishing the abstraction, realizing the meaning and studying from the formal point of view the meaning thus realized.

But what characterizes concrete psychology is that it does not leave the level of the drama and considers the story as a simple context that does not let us get into the inner life, but helps us understand a drama that takes place in our presence. The psychological fact cannot result either from *inner perception*, since the latter already implies the abandonment of the point of view properly psychological, and it is the least we can say, seeing that in the terms of the analysis it reveals itself as a pure illusion.

14. The psychological fact is not a perceptive theme but the result of a construction, it is easy to show that it is original and properly psychological without being inner, and that it is objective without being of matter or movement.

The drama is *original*. It has nothing to do with pure and simple matter or movement. The extent, movement or even energy, with all their states and all their processes, are not sufficient to establish the drama. For the drama implies the human being taken in his totality and considered as the center of a certain number of events that have a meaning, precisely because they relate to a first person.

It is the *meaning* related to a first person that radically distinguishes the psychological fact from all facts of nature. The originality of the psychological fact is given by the very existence of a properly human level and of the dramatic life of the individual that unfolds in it.

Only, the drama is not at all *inner*. The drama, to the extent to which it requires a place, unfolds in space as ordinary movement, as, in general, all the phenomena of nature. For the place where I am right now is not simply the place of my physiological life and of my biological life, it is also the place of my dramatic life, and, also, actions, crimes, madness, take place in space, as do breathing and inner secretions.

It is true, besides, that space can only contain the frame of the drama: the properly dramatic element is no longer spatial. Only, it is not *inner* either, since it is nothing other than *signification*. The latter does not and cannot take place anywhere; it is neither inner, nor outer, it is beyond or rather outside these possibilities, without this fact at all compromising its reality.

15. If the drama is neither outer, nor inner, in the spatial sense of these terms, it is however *outer* in the logical sense. For it is from the outside that the psychologist approaches the drama and

tries to understand its meaning and mechanism; the drama appears in front of him as might any reality; he must explore it as we explore nature. By the same token, the psychological fact is *objective*, even though this objectivity is not the one of outer perception. If the psychological fact is objective, it is not because it is expanded or because it is measurable, but because on the level of the empirical realism of science it is outside the act of the knowledge that accesses it; it is even, from this point of view, transcendent to it; it has its own dialectics and can be known only in a mediate way with the help of the themes of the story. In other words, the psychological fact is objective not because it is confused with the object of the sciences of nature and *is* what they are, but because it *behaves* in the same way in the presence of knowledge.

The themes of concrete psychology, without being experimental in the vulgar sense of the word, are, rightfully, universally accessible and verifiable. Anyone can, indeed, undertake the description and the analysis of the drama with the help of the method of the story.

16. We are right, therefore, to have asserted that concrete psychology represents the true synthesis between objective psychology and subjective psychology. It condones the one for not seeking a psychology that was not objective and the other for seeking to keep the character proper to psychology, but it condemns both for having sacrificed everything to what represents only one of the conditions of existence of positive psychology. It establishes at the same time what neither of them could do: an objective psychology, at the same time as being properly psychological.

The reality of the psychological fact as it is defined by concrete psychology is released of all metaphysical halo. Its affirmation does not imply the existence of a new essence in the realistic sense of the term, but simply that of a group of facts that do not take us back to the classic antithesis of mind and matter: psychology knows neither one, it only knows drama. Psychological facts show us a new world, but it is a world of knowledge and not a world of entities and *sui generis* processes; psychology does not give us access to a reality that can be opposed to or juxtaposed on nature. *Concrete psychology* does not know *psychic matter* and, what is more important, it is not satisfied with the purely formal negation of the thesis, but eliminates all the steps that produce it or derive from it. By the same token, *psychology stops being the science of inner life.*

17. The fact that concrete psychology is a synthesis between objective psychology and subjective psychology is an important statement when it concerns showing with precision its orientation among the tendencies of contemporary psychology. But it is, by the same token, only a classical virtue. The most important statement, because it interests not only the conditions of its birth, but the way in which, once born, it must orient itself, is that concrete psychology is a *psychology without inner life*. This is the fundamental virtue of concrete psychology; for it is essentially a psychology renouncing all the procedures with the help of which the human drama can be transformed into *inner life*. It is to this fact that it owes its actual fruitfulness, and its future depends on the consequence and vigor with which it will be capable of remaining in this path. For it is not difficult to distinguish human behavior from simply physiological and biological behavior. What is very difficult and will be until the disappearance of this generation raised in the idealogy of abstract psychology, is not to confuse the drama with the inner life, or rather not to answer all the questions that the drama asks us and which lead us to inner life.

18. To know the meaning of the drama, we must resort to the story of the subject. The content of the story, seen through classical psychology, implies the famous notions of images, perception, memory, will, emotion, etc., about which research is a dangerous temptation, even for a psychologist who conceives the necessity of concrete psychology. I close my eyes and I see the place of the Concorde with the Obelisque in the middle. The temptation to describe this vision and to make it an object of research is irresistible. And it is the same temptation that appears to all the *implications* of the story. Thus, it is at that moment that we must wary, for we must hold back on these implications.

Whatever the questions asked about the story, the psychologist must start by being interested only in its *content*; that is, its significa-tion. The signification of human behaviors can only be known because man expresses himself by speech, or if we prefer, because he thinks. But what interests the psychologist is no longer the thought in itself, it is not thought itself that he tries to grasp through its incarnations: he must not omit signification, to carry out this research, for that is precisely what is important to psychology.

19. In a general way, the forms of thought, the states of con-

sciousness, in short, the world in which introspective psychology moves, constitute an area that is situated beyond the drama. The psychologist must therefore be on guard. For the area in question, precisely because it is beyond the drama, constitutes, in relation with concrete psychology, a metapsychology where the psychologist, in the positive sense of the word, should not be led.

I make a gesture. I easily understand that its physiological mechanism has nothing to do with psychology. But, while accomplishing this gesture, I have thoughts that are like the spiritual duplicating of this gesture, and the temptation is great to go into the "disinterested" study of the "duplicating." It is then that we will need to understand that I am a *psychologist* and not a *metapsychologist*. The thoughts in themselves do not interest me. On the contrary, I can make, about this gesture, a *story* that gives me the sense of the gesture, its human and individual terms: that is what interests the psychologist.

The first duty of the concrete psychologist, therefore, is the acquisition of reservation toward metapsychology. But, the point of view of introspective psychology is so deeply rooted in us that we doubt the legitimacy of the effort necessary to go beyond it and to resist it. We need to know two things. First that sciences that are reputed as positive today became so only by sacrificing a certain number of great evidences. It is so that modern physics had to overcome the evidences of the Aristotelian vision of the world, and it is because of a training that has lasted centuries that the physician could get used to the quantitative vision of nature. It is the same for psychology. Victory over the metapsychology of the soul-substance was nothing, or, if we prefer, was only a start. What we need is victory over the metapsychology of inner life.

And, secondly, we need to know that by sacrificing the evidences in question, we only sacrifice false problems. For a part of the evidences to sacrifice is revealed, as we have tried to show that during the present work, and as we will continue to show in the following ones, as the effect of a *transcendental illusion*. There are indeed some which will be brought back, for they seem to be tied to real facts. It is thus, for example, that the *story* implies *memory*, and it seems impossible not to study the latter. But it is not the memory that interests the concrete psychologist, but the *remembrance* inasmuch as it sheds light on the drama, and since the latter is the first object of psychology, the memory itself only appears as a faraway supposition. We must first adopt the attitude of concrete psychology with all its consequences and only later approach certain parts of actual abstract psychology whose sacrifice appears today as arbitrary. It is only then that we will be able to see if the problems in question can or cannot have a concrete signification.

For the generation previous to the accomplishment of a scientific progress, victory over classical evidences seems impossible, and the ones who advocate its necessity are destined to fall back on it once in a while. It is because the transformation of the evidences is performed slowly but surely and, for the following generation, the problem is hardly there, and everything appears in a new light.

20. What the present research teaches us on concrete psychology still only concerns its necessity and vitality, but the idea that we have had of it until now must be expanded. This expansion cannot be either *a priori* or left to chance. It must be accomplished, on the one hand, by examining, with the help of this main theme that our present conception of concrete psychology constitutes, those tendencies of contemporary psychology that already denote a concrete orientation; and, on the other hand, by adopting the level that is given to us by the problems that derive from concrete psychology as we have shown it here.

21. Concrete psychology directs us first toward behaviorism. We have used in this work the term *behavior*, and we found it exactly to our taste. Furthermore, we have seen, from our introduction, that we attribute an essential importance to Watson's attempt. The reason is that behaviorism owes its existence to a concrete inspiration.

Let us forget the sensational side and the scandalous aspect of behaviorism; that is, the radical and ruthless negation of consciousness, of introspection, and of all introspective notions, to stop at this fundamental proposition: *The psychological fact is behavior.* If we later omit Watson's interpretation, which is entirely locked into the purely physiological conception of the pair "stimulus-response," we find that behavior is a segment of the life of the particular individual.

To assert that the psychological fact is behavior is to renounce the reconstitution of man by the combination of a group of concepts of more or less suspect origin such as sensation, memory, will, character, etc.; it is to assert the necessity of beginning with what is *truly real*, since behavior is nothing else but a *break* in the continual unfolding of the person's life. Watson also wants to start from the *whole* and reconstitute the concrete with the concrete, and not with the help of the abstract.

This is not an arbitrary interpretation of Watsonism. Watson himself is very well aware of the concrete character of the notion of *behavior*. We know how much he insists on the necessity of considering the organism *as a whole* and of renouncing the traditional breaks of psychology and physiology. But, to consider man *as a whole*, to study him in his concrete evolutions; that is, in his behaviors, to apply this point of view without failure, implies, whatever the final interpretation of the term *behavior*, a complete reform of the object and of the notions of classical psychology.

22. This is how the unexpected comparison that we make between behaviorism and psychoanalysis is justified. They both correspond to a revolt against abstraction which is the fundamental character of classical psychology: these are two attempts to introduce concrete analysis in a discipline that until now only knew abstract dreaming. Beyond biology, on the one hand, and beyond psychiatry, on the other, psychoanalysis and behaviorism join in an aversion for the abstract and in the effort to start again from what, on the particular level of each, appears to them as the concrete life of man.

Certainly, human behavior goes far beyond the Watsonian notion of *behavior*. Not only because this latter is not yet the drama, and can only be its frame, but also because the way the drama is *framed* contains all the degrees, going from an entirely *realistic* staging to a relation so far away that it has no more interest for us.

There is an important problem here: to expand the notion of human behavior by fixing with precision its content and its limits. But this can only be done by studying behaviorism and its different forms from the viewpoint of concrete psychology. This study will show us, besides, the extent to which what does not immediately relate to the drama can, however, be studied from the point of view of concrete psychology. For we certainly can find in contemporary, even official, psychology, results that go beyond realism and abstraction — if only in applied psychology. But to recognize them in a precise way, we would need to take all the content of current psychology and examine it from a new point of view. It is precisely for this research that the examination of what is alive and dead in behaviorism will be of essential importance.

It will show us if it is necessary, and in what sense, to establish a *general psychology*, at the same time as the frames and the notions that the concrete orientation of the latter supposes.

23. As our analyses have led us to use the notion of behavior, the notion of *signification* and even the one of *form* have played a fundamental role in our demonstrations. It is the drama, indeed, that we gave as object to concrete psychology. The drama essentially contains the notions of signification and even those of form. Our research is directed, on the one hand, toward Spranger's attempt and, on the other, toward Gestalt theory in general. There too, we find ourselves facing a tendency whose inspiration is clearly concrete, if only by the introduction of the point of view of meaning and by the abandonment of elementary analysis.

Only, the signification and the form, such as they intervene in concrete psychology, do not have at all the same meaning as with Spranger and with the followers of Gestalt theory, and, besides, we need to go further than the pure and simple abandonment of elementary analysis, for this abandonment must be at the same time the renouncing of metapsychology.

We expanded here neither the idea of signification, nor that of drama; we did not even determine their relations with precision. But these are the fundamental notions of concrete psychology. To define them, we need to study Gestalt theory.

24. The studies in question will give us, at the same time, another result that has no direct interest in the future of concrete psychology but in the critique of classical psychology.

The study of psychoanalysis has allowed us to isolate a certain number of fundamental steps of classical psychology. But for the critique to clarify the latter, it is indispensable to establish the *complete list* and the "finished" analysis of its steps. From this point of view the study of the two tendencies that we have just talked about is very interesting. For if each one of them participates, to a certain extent, in the concrete, the latter is revealed in aspects other than in psychoanalysis. We can then, either discover the classical steps that the study of psychoanalysis did not reveal, or expand in a new point of view the steps that we already know. And this expectation all the more legitimate, in that Gestalt theory, for example, is based precisely on the critique of this classical step, which is elementary analysis. We will then be concerned with knowing what the exact place of this approach in the hierarchy of the classical procedures is and if its negation is enough for the constitution of a really fruitful psychology — which will give us at the same time a critical instrument of first order to judge certain tendencies of Gestalt theory.

25. The present research unveils problems that will be resolved only in the ulterior studies that we have announced in our introduction. Something, however, is certain from now on: with concrete psychology, psychology enters a new path: *the study of concrete man*. This orientation, however, is new only with comparison to the preoccupations of official psychologists; it represents, in reality, only the return of psychology to this desire which is the main source of the confidence with which official psychology has lived until now. This desire is to know the human being. By consenting to make of this desire a scientific program, concrete psychology systemizes the great concrete tradition that has always fed literature, dramatic art and the science of wise men in the practical sense of the word. Only, concrete psychology, while having the same object, offers more than theater and literature: it offers *science*. This is how we will end up with a psychology that is not, like classical psychology, less, but which is more than the teachings of the ordinary observation of man.

26. The development of psychology has great surprises in store for us, for the history of a science cannot be guessed *a priori*. Psychoanalysis is a beginning, it is only a beginning, and we must, now that light is shed on its true essence, pursue research by considering a new point of view. Behaviorism and Gestalt theory having to be almost entirely reformed, we can say that in the technical point of view a lot has to be done. Technical progress will have bearing on the way in which we need to conceive the foundations. But what is certain is that any turning back is impossible. Psychology will never be able to go back to realism and to abstraction: the problem is now shown in a totally new area. And it will never be able to go back, either, to physiological psychology, or to introspective psychology; two obstacles stop it from doing this: behaviorism and psychoanalysis. In a word, and whatever the imprecision of our technical formulas and the unpleasant resounding of the formulas of this kind may be: *metapsychology* has lived its life, and the history of *psychology* is beginning.

Notes

Notes to Introduction

1. Warren's manual is significant with regard to this.

2. Let it be understood once and for all that by the term *drama* we mean a fact and that we leave out of the account any romantic connotations of this word. We ask the reader to get used to this meaning and to forget its "moving" signification.

3. Psychoanalysis is an exception.

4. Cf. Lebensformen, 5th ed. Halle, 1925.

5. Freud, for example, takes on the responsibility of bringing back psychoanalysis to classical psychology, as we will see later.

6. The *Materiaux* is planned in three volumes. After the present volume, there will be another volume on Gestalt theory, with a chapter on phenomenology; the third one will treat behaviorism and its different forms with a chapter on applied psychology.

7. "Einige Bemerkungen über den Begriff des Unbewussten in der Psychoanalyse," in *Kleine Schriften zur Neurosenlehre*, Folge, 4:165, Vienna, 1922.

Notes to Chapter One

1. The references that have no indication of a title relate to the French translation of the *Traumdeutung* (translation by M.I. Meyerson, Paris, Alcan, 1927).

2. Cf. below, 57 ff.

3. Cf. chapter 2.

4. We will use from now on the term "I" to indicate the first person and not for the technical meaning it has with Freud. Cf. *Das Ich und das Es*, Vienna, 1923.

5. Lebensformen, 5. (5th ed., Halle Niemeyer, 1925.)

6. Lebensform, 5.

7. Cf. below, and especially 236.

8. Cf. beginning of chapter 2, and chapter 5.

9. See further, chapter 2.

10. One can imagine that I have not communicated everything that came to my mind during the work of interpretation. (*Note from Freud*)

11. What is more, there remains with Freud a wavering on the question: some exceptions have been admitted. But the sense of Freud's preference is very clear.

12. "If necessary," because in most cases, there is only pure and simple fanticizing. Cf. our chapter 2: "Introspection and the Psychoanalytic Method."

13. We admit, to simplify the discussion, that it is really experience that has answered the question. Cf. chapter 2.

14. Except in "dogmatic" writings, like *Jenseits des Lustprincips or Das Ich und das Es*, and in general the writings of "metapsychology," but, here again, the analytical facts largely intervene.

15. There is also a whole *objective psychoanalysis* that interprets autobiographies, intimate diaries, etc.

16. Notably by establishing a parallel between the psychoanalytic method and introspection.

Notes to Chapter Two

1. There is in classical psychology a method that we can be tempted to compare with the Freudian method: it is the method of questionnaires. This method can effectively give objective results. But what lacks to those who use it, is precisely a concrete notion of psychology: the questions asked being abstract, so are the answers. And the method could only give valid results to the extent to which those who used it were concrete in spite of themselves.

2. We will only talk later of the way that classical psychology treats the *story*. But we will easily see that everything we will say about it will apply equally to the *vision*.

3. We know that in the past we went further, and we had admitted to a complete parallelism between language and thought. But whatever are the refinements of the more recent theories, we will always find there the model of the procedure that we describe.

4. Cf. further, chapter 4, 9, p. 206 sq.

5. Cf. below, 100.

6. It is in the *Essay* that they need to be taken systematically.

7. I do not insist on this problem, because book 2 of the "Materials for the Critique of the Foundation of Psychology" is precisely on Spranger, and, in general on the Gestalt theory.

Notes to Chapter Three

1. Given the orientation of our developments, here we explicitly answer the second question.

2. As Freud compares consciousness to a sense organ, we no longer need to expand on the question of relativity.

3. Cf. below, chapter 4, section 5, sqq.

4. It is true that in the recent development of his theories, Freud comes back to the problem of repression, and we find then some developments that come close to the exigencies that we just expressed. But these developments only stress the conflict between the abstraction and the concrete. Cf. chapter 5, section 3, 236 ff.

5. Cf. above, 136. Scherner's theory.

6. The italics are ours.

7. Cf. also: *Das Ich und das Es*, 19 sqq.

Notes to Chapter Four

1. The analyses of this chapter continue in volumes 2 and 3 of the *Materiaux*, and again in a systematic way in the *Essay*.

2. *Vorlesungen uber den Traum*, 117 (Vienna, 1922).

3. *Das Ich und das Es*, 10 (Vienna, 1923).

4. 104–05.

5. *Das Ich und das Es*, 10–11.

6. *Vorlesungen uber den Traum*, 11.

7. *Das Ich und das Es*, 11–12.

8. *Das Ich und das Es*, 11.

9. To indicate the role of formalism in the deformation of the facts, which become, thus, proofs of the unconscious, is only, after what we have said about it in chapter 3, a game. We develop this point only for clarity.

10. We must remember that the fact that whether the story is done "internally" or "publicly" has no importance.

11. That we touched on in passing, 174 ff.

Notes to Chapter Five

1. Chapter 4, 6.

2. Cf. the texts that we have quoted [G. Politzer].

3. Cf. for the texts, above, Chapter 3, section 2, beginning, 105–06; section 3, 115, and in general the last section of the *Traumdeutung*.

4. We are not giving the list of *all* the concrete notions and explanations that are found with Freud, but examples, or rather *models* able to show that concrete notions and explanations indeed exist in psychoanalysis. That is why we talk of neither "transfer," nor of "introjection," nor the "inferiority complex" of A. Adler, etc.

5. Cf. however further, 236.

6. Cf. for example *Traumdeutung*, 4th ed. German, p. 114 sq.)

7. *Zur Einleitung des Narzismus*, and *Group Psychology and Analysis of the Ego*.

8. *Group Psychology and Analysis of the Ego*, chap. 8.

9. *Das Ich und das Es*, chap. e, especially 32 sqq.

10. Cf. above, chap. 1, section 4, 52 ff.

Index

171